D0255278

Don't Miss Love

STEVEN BATCHELOR

Excerpts from the following used by permission:

The Holy Bible, New International Version by International Bible Society. 1984. Zondervan Publishing House. All rights reserved.

The Message: the Bible in Contemporary Language. Peterson, Eugene H. NAVPress, 2005. Excerpts used by permission.

Mere Christianity by C.S.Lewis, C.S. Lewis Pte. LTD. 1952.

The Bell by Iris Murdoch, Penguin Random House. 1999.

Wooden: A Lifetime of Observations and Reflections On and Off the Court by John Wooden. McGraw-Hill. 1997.

"The ultimate lesson all of us have to learn is unconditional love, which includes not only others but ourselves as well" by Elisabeth Kübler-Ross in *The Wheel of Life*. Bantam Books. 1997.

Copyright © 2018 Steven Batchelor
All rights reserved.
ISBN-13: 9781985585355
ISBN-10: 1985585359

DEDICATION

To my dear sister Mary Lou Fore. In her short fifty-three years, she never missed an opportunity to show love and grace.

CONTENTS

PROLOGUE

Early in the evening of February 18, 2017, my wife and I returned from a trip to our nation's capital. We took off from Reagan National Airport and chased the sunset to our home in Oregon. As we flew over the Midwest, the darkening ground below revealed few details save a scattering of dim lights from the occasional small town slumbering almost seven miles below. But in time, there was a prominent landmark-the mighty Mississippi River. It shone as a glimmering ribbon against a black velvet canvas as the setting sun, far to the West, reflected from its flat surface.

As I looked down at its winding path, God reminded me of the many unforeseen twists and turns my life had taken over the previous couple of years. Only from this elevated vantage point could I see life's many changes in direction. From the surface, all a person can see is his path bending away, out of view. He must wait to see what lies ahead, and before long, even that too would change.

Two years prior to our trip east, I had come to a major bend in the river. I was diagnosed with cancer. From that point on, my life took one turn after another, and each turn was game-changing. I saw how facing death changes the way a person looks at life. I had resolved to meet the obstacles head-on with determination and a lot of prayer. I'd been-and remained-convinced that God would use my disease for his good, that I would be a shining example of his healing power and grace. I looked hard for every glimmer of hope that my life would be spared. I looked deep inside myself for the strength to persevere the difficult treatment and its many challenging side effects.

Yet despite all my yearning for understanding, for strength, I found something I hadn't asked for, something I wasn't even aware I needed: love. Every treatment, every disappointment, every victory brought me face to face with the boundless power of God's unconditional love. Through my entire journey, love has met me at every bend and carried me through to the next.

And the more I see love in my own life, the more I notice the lack of it in our culture, in our world. Love seems to have been replaced by the isolation of our ever quickening pace and our obsession with technology. Love's purity and prominence are becoming an afterthought.

This book could change that. Just as love has brought peace and understanding to my life, it can do the same for anyone who seeks it. Love is capable of softening the hard edges of our lives like nothing else. Love can unite our hearts with a singular beat of compassion and empathy. This book is about love's purity and simplicity. It's also about love's power, living in your heart now, awaiting your call. Author and speaker Leo Buscaglia said, "Love is life. And if you miss love, you miss life." Turn the pages ahead and you'll see what you might be missing.

1

Love Is

"Love is a little word. People make it big."
Anonymous

My life was turned upside down when I was diagnosed with throat cancer. This happened on June 20th, 2015. During the remaining summer and fall of 2015, I underwent aggressive treatment that included seven weeks of daily radiation and weekly chemotherapy. The radiation treatment alone made it inadvisable for me to expose the radiated areas of my body, namely my neck and shoulders, to direct sunlight. My wife, Kim, and I are not the type of people to sit around indoors on a beautiful sunny day. Since it was fairly early in my treatment and my energy was still good, we decided to take our boat out for one last ski trip. To make it possible for me to be outside for an extended period of time, I decided to purchase the most logical head covering, something that would not only provide shade, but have some personality too: a cowboy hat.

It was a bit surprising to me to discover that the only western store in our home town of Portland, Oregon is located smack-dab in the middle of downtown. I drove there and surprisingly found a parking spot right in front of the store. As I started to walk towards the front door, something out of the corner of my eye caught my attention. To my right, a couple of hundred feet away, a group of youngish-looking people were sitting on the sidewalk. Even from that distance, I could tell they were most likely part of

Portland's ever-growing homeless population. Now despite what you may have heard about Portland, it does not rain twenty-four hours a day, three hundred sixty-five days a year. In fact, the summers can get downright toasty. On this occasion, it was approaching ninety degrees and it was barely noon. I decided to see if there was anything I could do, considering the fact that the sidewalk was slowly being transformed into a short order grill-and they were the unfortunate sizzling meat. As I got close, I realized these folks were not prepared for the conditions.

Five individuals, and one small dog (surprisingly, for Portland, it wasn't a pit bull), were bivouacked on the sidewalk in front of a fairly typical downtown convenience store, the kind with every window covered by advertising posters for beer, smokes and other "necessities."

"Good morning." I approached and stopped in front of them. "How are you guys? Is there anything you need?" They answered almost as one and told me some water would be very welcome.

"How about food? You must be hungry."

Their impromptu "leader" said, "Anything would be very kind." The rest nodded in agreement. The dog looked pretty listless. Then I noticed they also had a cat.

"Okay, I'll see what I can find for you in here." I opened the door to the small market.

On the crowded shelves, I found a typical collection of not so nutritious items, most of which were exactly what these people didn't need. Eventually, I found some sandwiches and large bottles of chilled water. I even picked up a small bag of dog food. I had to make a couple of trips to the check-out counter before I had everything ready.

After I'd assembled my stash next to the cash register and pulled out my wallet, the clerk asked, "Are you buying this for those people in front of my store?"

"Yes I am. They don't seem to have much of anything." I handed him my debit card.

"Those people hurt my business." His voice was not friendly. "You buy them food, they don't leave. All they're doing is making people not come in." His tone didn't stop him from ringing-up my purchase of what were no doubt outrageously overpriced provisions.

With as much empathy as I could register, I said, "I understand why you feel this way. But it's hard for me to walk away from people who clearly need help when I'm able to do something. I hope you can understand my point of view as well."

He frowned, "You're not helping me. You're only helping them."

I gathered my purchase in a couple of plastic bags, and with a smile on my face, turned towards the front door. I walked out to some very grateful people. I can only assume the provisions made the dog and cat happy too.

Portland, like most cities, has no shortage of homeless people living on its streets. I'm aware that feeding these people, especially when they congregate directly in front of a business, can perpetuate the problem and cause a more paying clientele to stay away. And, just like other cities, Portland does a great job of providing relief for its homeless population. I volunteer at one of the missions. But on that day, at that place, my motivation was more immediate. These people needed assistance and I was in a position to give it. Clearly, I could also have suggested they relocate to one of the many shelters or kitchens more suited to meet their needs, but my goal was compassion, not correction.

That story is an example of the kind of pre-meditated love that I am suggesting can have a very real impact on us and others. Although I'd done things similar to this in the past, this time in particular got me thinking about how love, in its purest form, should be dispensed more liberally by more people. Later that evening, the term "Don't Miss Love" came to me as a condensed way to say what I'd been thinking. It made me wonder how many times I'd been in a similar situation and either ignored the need, or justified a way to not get involved. The more I thought about it, the more I realized this notion of being disconnected from the obvious could have much broader implications.

Giving food and water to someone clearly in need of help is one thing. But what about giving a simple smile and nod to acknowledge someone crossing your path? Should I develop a list of instances that qualify for my attention and loving action? Should the list include a graduated scale of love? A nod could be one star; a nod and a smile, two stars. Maybe giving someone food and water would earn ten stars. Obviously, this would be ridiculous and undermine any spontaneity that must be a part of living a life of love. To repeat the old British idiom: "In for a penny, in for a pound," which just means if I'm in for some of it, I'm in for all of it. Or to put it into context, if I am going to pour out love to someone, I ought to bring a bucket, not an eyedropper.

The word love has conjured up a plethora of definitions over the millennia. I wouldn't even begin to think I could come up with a universally acceptable definition. Love means different things to different people. In fact, love often means different things to the same person. When someone says, "I love this pizza," hopefully they don't mean love in the same way they love their wife and children. If they do, I recommend good family counseling, right after they send me the name of that pizza joint. To be sure, the word love is often used fast and loose:

"Dude, I love this car."

"I absolutely love your new haircut."

"I love this show."

And from the classic beer commercial; "I love you man!" ("You can't have my Bud Light, Johnny!").

Fortunately, the ancients, those who first labored to define love, focused on truer forms of love than the feelings we have for light beer. First, they had *philia*, or brotherly love. Philadelphia was named after this emotion. *Storge* was the love between immediate family members. Granted, *philia* and *storge* are so similar, the lines between them are easily blurred.

Another kind of love that deserves mentioning is eros love. This love, named after the Greek god of love, has evolved into a kind of sketchy meaning for sexual love, or to put it bluntly, sexual lust in general. Our enlightened culture has taken a word originally intended to define a normal, healthy sexual relationship between two committed lovers, and in some cases, even as a broader term for the enjoyment of the aesthetic beauty of art and nature, and transformed it into a word that is now most commonly associated with eroticism. For me, eroticism shouldn't play any part in formulating our game plan to extend ourselves towards others, (no pun intended).

As part of my research for this book, I randomly asked people what love meant to them. My only clarification was that I was not referring to romantic love. I asked men and women from a wide spectrum of ages and cultures the same question. The predominant response was consistent and very encouraging. Here are a few of the responses:

"Accepting someone for everything they are."
- Hannah

"Love to me is a person – Jesus Christ. Love gives a purpose and a hope."
- Janice

"Love has no conditions."
- Sharon

"Love is *Agape*. Love is about compromise."

- Stephen

"Love changed me. Love is a choice beyond will power."

- Randy

"Love is made in God's image."

- Mark

"It gives me a tingling feeling." (When I reminded him I was not referring to romantic love, he said, "I know, but it just makes me feel good to be nice to other people.")

- Joseph

It's easy to see a theme in these responses. People, who have never met each other or had the opportunity to arrive at a consensus, seemed to have the same general opinion of what love is. The predominant theme? Love is something to be given or shared with someone else. It is not a thing to possess in order to keep for one's self. The other theme I see from these responses is that most people believe love shouldn't have conditions. Love is pure, unencumbered acceptance, and if you accept someone, you accept all of the person.

This brings us to the mother of all loves: *Agape* (ah-gah-pey) love or charity (*caritas* in Latin). *Agape* is the summation of every virtue. It is the inexhaustible aquifer from which all expressions of love are drawn. If it were a tree, it would be colossal. It would tower over everything else and would be seen from everywhere by every person. From it would hang the fruit of everything good and worthy, everything beautiful, everything pure. It would bear fruit in all seasons and never run out. Its fruit would always be ripe and sweet. Augustine said, "No fruit is good which does not grow from the root of love (*caritas*)." Thomas Aquinas tells us there is no virtue without *caritas*.

Ultimately, *agape* love is characterized as the love of God. Christianity's very foundation is rooted in God's unconditional love for mankind; "For

God so loved the world, that he gave his one and only son, that whoever believes in him shall not perish but have eternal life." (John 3:16, NIV). This famous verse from the Gospel of John sums up the entire content of the Bible.

I realize there are people reading this book who either do not agree with the Bible or simply don't believe in God. Many people have completely different opinions of where love came from. Talk to an evolutionary psychologist about love and he or she may tell you it is simply a psychological response to the right kind of stimuli. There is no more spirituality behind it than there is behind any other emotion. We all just come pre-wired for love.

You don't have to look very hard to find a book supporting this humanistic belief, but the book you are holding is not one of them. I believe, as do millions of others, that God is love, which means love is God. They are inseparable. I most certainly agree our human physiology requires some sequence of electrochemical events for us to experience any emotion. This is an indisputable scientific fact. After all, we are an exquisitely designed structure made up of billions of cells. Everything that happens in our bodies has its origin in a physiological event—from our hearts beating to our fingers moving to our emotions churning.

How our physical bodies process emotions is a fact of science, but these facts don't diminish how emotions shape our lives and the way we interact with other people. I believe love is God's first and greatest gift, because the Bible tells us he is love. More than that, I believe love is humanity's preeminent emotion-in that its has the unique capacity to unite us, to get to the heart of what is best about all of us. The love we don't want to miss is *agape* love. It is charitable love, it is divine love, it is pure love and it is love with but one expectation-that it be received as genuine.

7

There are a couple of important things to know about this kind of love. First, all love, by definition, requires an object. Love without an "object of affection" never lands. And no matter how much sincere joy and compassion love may contain, it's meaningless when it has no destination. In his classic book, *Mere Christianity*, C.S. Lewis explains this as no one else can.

"All sorts of people are fond of repeating the Christian statement that 'God is love'. But they seem not to notice that the words 'God is love' have no real meaning unless God contains at least two Persons. Love is something that one person has for another person. If God was a single person, then before the world was made, He was not love. Of course, what these people mean when they say that God is love is often something quite different: they really mean 'Love is God'. They really mean that our feelings of love, however and wherever they arise, and whatever results they produce, are to be treated with great respect. Perhaps they are: but that is something quite different from what Christians mean by the statement 'God is love'. They believe that the living, dynamic activity of love has been going on in God forever and has created everything else.

And that, by the way, is perhaps the most important difference between Christianity and all other religions: that in Christianity God is not a static thing—not even a person—but a dynamic, pulsating activity, a life, almost a kind of drama. Almost, if you will not think me irreverent, a kind of dance."

The second point to remember is that this type of love is, as C.S. Lewis puts it, "an affair of the will." It begins with our willful decision to act charitably towards another person whether we like them or not. Love, in this sense, is not an emotion, but a decision. We choose to treat another with compassion, or any other virtue, not because we feel affection or love necessarily, but because it is our choice. Perhaps you've heard the management approach telling you to treat people like they're already acting the way you want them to act. In a way, this is the same thing. When we decide to treat people as if we already like them, eventually, most people will act as if they are liked and that you care about them. Again, C.S. Lewis in *Mere Christianity*:

"Do not waste time bothering whether you 'love' your neighbour; act as if you did. As soon as we do this we find one of the great secrets. When you are behaving as if you loved someone, you will presently come to love him."

Here's another example. A friend of mine is an elementary school teacher. At the beginning of each school year, many of the teachers and staff choose to participate in a sort of game called "Secret Pal." Each person is given the name of another participant. As the year goes by, they subtly learn the likes and dislikes of their secret pal, then every month they give their pal a small gift that compliments what they have learned about this other person. My friend has taught for a long time, and since she began, she's had some secret pals who weren't necessarily her favorite at the beginning of the school year. But an interesting thing has happened every year; by the end of the year, she grew to like her pal, someone she may not have cared for in the beginning, simply by getting to know them.

Willfully or not, my friend ended up in a charitable relationship with someone she may never have approached at first. Though we may never have secret pals, we can approach others with the same mindset. Given the choice, wouldn't it be wise to approach others like my teacher did her secret pal? If we choose to serve people, choose to get to know people, choose to care about people, over time, we will find we love those people. In that way, we could all choose to jump to "loving" conclusions.

We want to love more, don't we? And the world supplies a nearly unlimited number of possible recipients for our love, every person on the planet. If we use C.S. Lewis's analogy, our life of love is made up of different dance partners we encounter throughout our journey. First, we have to decide if we even want to go to the dance in the first place, and then we need to be open to our partners. When the music starts, the steps may be different each time, but love's music will always be the same.

Friends, we are missing love, and the kind of love that will become the catalyst for improving ourselves and others is best exemplified by God himself. The next chapter will help us identify it in ourselves. We are all pre-programmed for love, but there's no guarantee we have made the leap from using it as a verb rather than a noun. In fact, we may be horrible at it. But we can change that. For some of us, we may just need to redirect or tweak some of our habits. Others may have no experience as a loving person. But if we are willing, love will allow us to breathe fresh, new life into ourselves.

You don't live in a vacuum. You are surrounded by people who want and need (even if they don't realize it) loving connections. Why can't you make some of those connections? It may seem disconcerting or even weird at first, but I assure you, after a while, loving others will have an unexpected, positive impact on your days.

"Love is a little word. People make it big." What at first appears to be a minor, perhaps even insignificant, emotion has the power to become very big when we allow it to work through us to reach others. This single word, love, can become a bridge of hope and unity that gains strength and becomes much larger than when it began. Even constructing the Empire State Building began with a draftsman's single mark on a piece of paper. Right now, you are somewhere in the midst of love's process of making you a better person. Will you see it in yourself? The next chapter will show you that you already possess the essential ingredients to be a loving person.

1. Again, not in reference to romantic love, write your own definition of love.

2. Must the term *agape* love only be associated with Christian love? Why or why not?

3. Do you agree with C.S. Lewis when he says charitable love is an act of the will? Why or why not?

4. Must true, unconditional love be associated with God (or a Supreme Being)? Why or why not?

5. Are we born with the capacity to love unconditionally? Explain your answer.

6. Share with your group your definition of love. Can you all agree on a single definition? Write it below.

7. Discuss the quote at the beginning of this chapter.

2
It's In There

"We can only learn to love by loving."
Iris Murdoch

Sometimes a simple drive to work can be quite revealing. My wife and I live on the west side of Portland in the community of Cedar Mill. We're separated from downtown by the one-thousand-foot-high West Hills. Since my job is downtown, every day I have to choose between a very congested freeway, or a somewhat circuitous, although scenic, route through these hills that eventually drops me pretty close to my office. One morning while driving in, I got stuck behind a rather large box van heading in the same direction. The curves didn't allow the driver to maintain a pace anywhere near what I would normally make. After just a couple of these curves, the truck pulled to the side of the road and allowed me to pass. Somewhat astonished, I made a mental note of the company markings on the side of the van.

After I arrived at work and had settled into my daily routine, I Googled the company and got their phone number. During my first break, I called. "Good morning. I just wanted to tell you about something that happened this morning with one of your trucks while I was driving in today."

"Oh, I'm sorry. Can you tell me what happened?" The man on the phone had an understandably concerned tone.

"Oh no, it's nothing like that. I called to tell you how thankful I am for what your driver did." I went on to explain what had happened and how much I appreciated it.

"You won't believe this," the man said, "but I was riding in that very truck this morning and I remember exactly when that happened. I'm in sales and the company likes us to do ride-alongs once in a while."

"You're kidding!" I said. "This sure is a coincidence."

"I'll tell that driver you called and what you said. We don't get calls like this very often. It won't be wasted. Thanks!"

Some people may not call either the driver's actions or my phone call an act of love. All the guy did was pull over so I could pass. But it didn't stop there. When I called to thank him, I completed a two-way process. I'd like to believe the driver wasn't just trying to impress the salesman and that pulling over so I could pass is his typical behavior. My call only reinforced what he already knew. As minor as this event may appear, it embodies an act of love.

As I've already said, I believe all of us have the beating pulse of love within. We have all received love and given love to some degree during our lives. Typically, the first memories we could attribute to love come from our parents and family. No matter how long it's been since the beginnings of what we remember as love, there was a natural purity and comfort that filled us, that connected us to the giver. Unfortunately, some of us have received inadequate and perhaps even misguided love. During our formative years, our exposure to the essence of love and the quality of that love has been dependent on the giver. If the giver has a healthy understanding of what love is and is capable of showing it, a person is more likely to understand what love is, what it means to love and to be loved. On the other hand, I've met people who can't remember a single time in their lives when a parent ever told them that they loved them. How would that person define love? Studies have proved that orphans who are not nurtured with a loving touch can experience severe emotional issues. But regardless of how we describe our loving foundation, we all have some degree of understanding about what love is and how it can affect us. We're all born with the capacity to give and receive love. Even if it feels foreign to us, when the circumstances are right, that supreme of all emotions will begin to percolate. This will happen as surely as we'll experience anger and, perhaps, even hatred. Love and hate are emotions we all possess, but love will always rise to the occasion. Love will never undermine other virtues. Pure love will never be wrong. Love is in you and me to stay as surely as our hearts beat. Our lives will be shaped by what love will be and do in each of us.

It's one thing to love people who love you back, to love your family and friends. But have you tried loving strangers or people who aren't nice to you? At first, it can seem challenging. But you more than likely have already begun the process. Maybe it was helping someone pickup something they had dropped or a time you gave a few dollars to someone who was a bit short at the grocery check out. How did you feel afterwards? Did you feel better? I'm betting the act made you feel pretty good. Imagine if you made loving strangers a part of your daily life. Jesus Christ said, "You are far happier giving than getting." (Acts 20:35, *The Message*). Something very emotionally satisfying happens when we give to someone else with no expectation of receiving anything in return.

A slight variation of this should be pointed out. Every year, our country spends billions of dollars on gifts we will give to each other at Christmas. With very few exceptions, the satisfying feeling we get by doing something kind for someone else, or giving to someone in need, doesn't seem to translate during the Christmas holiday. This annual day of giving comes with expectations that counteract what Jesus said about giving. We give because we feel obligated. We give because to do otherwise would be inadequate or even rude. We give because we get. Do you even remember what you got for Christmas last year? Me, neither. What I do remember is the donation we made that helped bring fresh water to a village in Africa.

When love is the motivation behind the kindness, it will never be confused with an obligation. Love brings an inherent joy when we help someone, whether it's by sacrificing our time or our resources. It is the act that is the gift, love being passed from one heart to another. Whether the gift is time or a new toaster, the essence of the love that motivated it in the first place remains. I assure you, the next time you show a kindness to someone else, if you're paying attention to what is happening in your heart, you'll notice it quickens an extra beat. That feeling-that's joy and it's just one of the fruits of love.

For me, there is a whole other reason to reach out to others. It must be how I'm wired, but I can't come in close contact with another person and not acknowledge them. When I walk down the sidewalk, I always make eye contact with people and, if their eyes meet mine, I smile and say hello. It is the rare occasion when I don't at least get a smile or some kind of acknowledgment in return. Every time this happens, my day seems a little brighter. I don't feel isolated. As you might imagine, it's becoming more difficult for this to happen these days when more and more people are transfixed staring at their smart phones. People are just as likely to unwittingly crash into each other as to make eye contact.

Speaking of technology, this is a good time for a brief stint on my soapbox. As much as I dislike the ways modern technology has effected how we communicate and our interpersonal interactions-especially when pared with the ever-increasing varieties of social media-it looks like it's only going to get worse. What was once a convenient form of communication has become the very platform from which many function on a near twenty-four-hour basis. And, unfortunately, this is not just lessening the possibility of stranger-to-stranger contact, it also permeates relationships with our friends and loved ones. A good example of this is when you see two people sitting across the table from each other in a restaurant and both spend the entire time staring at their phones. Even if they are each have a stimulating "conversation" on their phones, it is still short-circuiting what should be happening with the person sitting directly across the table. Face-to-face conversation nurtures and helps maintain relationships. not to mention the opportunities for creative discussion and spontaneity. Why go out to eat only to stare at your phone? Or have you ever seen a parent so wrapped up in what's happening on his phone that he completely ignores his child? Both of these instances illustrate a disconnect between one person and another. If you are in the presence of a friend or loved one, how is spending most of the time interacting with technology showing them you care about them and are glad to be with them?

On the positive side, there seems to be a silver lining starting to shine through. People are starting to realize the adverse affect technology is having on us. There are restaurants that ban the use of cell phones and many public assemblies ban, or at least discourage their use. I admit our technology has improved some facets our lives, mine as well. I take advantage of the convenience of sending text messages and emails to friends and family frequently. It's easy and saves time. But for what? What should I do with the time I save? I guess I could say it gives me more quality time with my family and friends. The reality is it's not so much about time, but that every time I send a text rather than actually calling the person and having a conversation, I feel like I too am succumbing to the pull of technology. Everyone lives a different life from everybody else and how we choose to utilize modern technology is obviously up to us. But I believe we should place limitations, or at least establish some priorities, on how we communicate with others. This is especially important if they are sitting three feet away. If it really is better to give than receive, perhaps just giving our undivided attention is the best thing we could give.

My friend Rich, recently told me about how, after attending a business seminar, he took the time to hand write a letter of thanks to each of the speakers from the seminar. He said every single speaker responded with appreciation. I doubt sending even individual emails would have carried the same weight. The personal connection of Rich's letters really made a difference. Should we do this every time we say thanks to someone? Of course not, but when every thing we say is read on a screen, words can lose their meaning and significance.

Modern technology has, without doubt, improved the quality of our lives in ways few of us ever could have imagined. I can't tell you how much I've welcomed texts from someone telling me they're praying for me about an upcoming cancer treatment. That simply wouldn't have been an option not that long ago. But regardless of the convenience, I think we need to be wise about technology. Let's make sure we take advantage of every opportunity to look someone in the face, smile and ask them how they're doing. Okay, enough about technology.

Even though I am predisposed to interact with people I meet during my day, since I began writing this book, I've been paying even closer attention to what happens when two people cross paths. Perhaps I've been more proactive in how often I exchange greetings. One of the pleasant side effects has been that greeting people seems to be adding a new dimension to my day. It's like each friendly encounter becomes a high point that was missing before. The more this happens, the more pleasantly my day goes. This, of course, can also include the interactions occurring as a part of my actual job. It's really starting to feel like a win-win situation. It might sound corny and simple, but the old saying, "If it feels good, do it," fits here. For me, it feels good to have friendly encounters. The fruit of this approach has made a difference I am really enjoying. I'm going to keep doing it and see how good it can get.

Why else should we embrace a more open and loving approach? Because it's the right thing to do. Love has been installed on your hard drive. You can't erase it. Love is here to stay. If you're willing to acknowledge our supreme emotion exists within you, wouldn't you want to make the most of it? Love is meant to be shared with others. When you release it from yourself to someone else, it fulfills its purpose. Remember, we're talking about *agape* love. This is very important to keep in mind because if we lose track of the kind of love we're attempting to resurrect in our lives, what we're trying to do won't work. Let me explain.

Obviously, in the case of romantic, or eros love, it would be nearly impossible to open yourself emotionally to strangers. People get locked up for that. Brotherly, familial or spousal love would be inappropriate for someone you may barely know and most definitely inappropriate towards a stranger. Only unconditional, unwarranted love can be applied to everyone, including strangers.

I believe we were designed to offer *agape* love naturally. Why else would unconditional love exist? So, if we agree the unconditional love that has been part of our DNA since the beginning is real and exists in all of us, we must admit it's not there to keep bottled up. Love is the best thing about all of us, but it is designed to be shared. If we can learn to share it liberally

19

without qualification, our remodeling process will begin from the inside out. We will become more comfortable with ourselves and others.

Imagine you're going to a party. Maybe you'll see some people you don't know. You may be more likely to mingle with strangers and get to know them. It's possible some of these new acquaintances could become good friends in time. During the course of your life, assuming you don't knock over too many punch bowls, you'll presumably attend a fair number of parties and, within this scenario, have multiple reasons to step outside your comfort zone with other people.

Now let's say you're at a gathering and, during the course of congenial conversation with a new acquaintance, discover you have unknowingly been crossing each other's paths for years while walking to work or riding the same bus everyday. What if you had met them sooner under different circumstances? Why did it take a party? Sure, it's easier to make a new friend at a party than while sitting on a bus. But does it always have to be the perfect scenario to open yourself up to other people?

The same dynamic occurs at most every party. Some folks you know, some you don't. The moment you step out and make friendly contact with one of those strangers, you're doing the very thing I am suggesting we could do when we're not at a party. We can do it any time we want. Meeting others doesn't have to be motivated by a need to make more friends. If you strike up a conversation at a party, you do it because it's what people do at parties. It would be crazy to try and pre-qualify every person you ever talk to as to whether or not you might want them as a friend. The same principle applies when you're on the street. Trying to pre-qualify someone by whether or not they are "friend worthy" is a crap shoot that should be far removed from our impetus to project love outside ourselves. If we make a new friend in the process, all the better. Even that is part of our main goal in being a more loving person.

Now, with something inside worth sharing, how can we know if we're even capable of becoming overtly loving on a new and different level? We have all heard the saying; "Practice makes perfect." In this case, I would revise that to say, "Practice makes it more genuine and a bit easier each time." While I believe love in itself is perfect, I don't believe there is always a perfect way to apply it. What could approach perfection in one case, may be way off in another. With practice, we can become more comfortable with the process. In some ways, it's the same as anything else that's new to us whether it's learning to play guitar or make scrambled eggs. The more you do it, the better you get. However, one distinct difference in learning how to share love is that, unlike learning to play a guitar, we already possess the ability within. We love because we are human. You don't play a guitar simply because you're human, and no matter how hard you try, you may never be any good at it.

I've long been convinced that everybody is good at something. Remember the guy in the movie, Deliverance, who played the banjo? Even from the depths of his inbred, solitary existence, he'd been blessed with a great ability to play that instrument. He may have been a banjo savant for all we know. And consider the hours and hours of devoted training and practice necessary to realize the awesome reward of becoming an Olympic athlete. For me, unless building birdhouses becomes an Olympic event, I'll never stand on that podium. I can play a guitar though.

What are you good at? If you're like many people, you possess hidden abilities you've yet to discover. But most people likely have something they wish they could do better. Sometimes the things they would like to do better are based on need more than desire. Maybe there is a skill that would improve their monthly income-or open their personal world to a particularly appealing group. Others would like to master a skill or ability just because it looks interesting or they feel it would be fulfilling or entertaining.

Love fits both of these criteria; we can want to become better at it because it will improve the quality of our lives and because it will add a missing dimension to our lives. In either case, when we embrace the need and pursue it, we will become better at it. When we become better, we will begin to use it more frequently and it evolves into a self-perpetuating part of who we are. When this happens, we are on the path to fulfilling the loving nature we were meant to have all along. The more of us who are willing, the better our world becomes. Making our world a better place starts inside each of us, one at a time.

Finally, just in case none of the reasons I have given for why we should become a more open and loving society and world are valid enough, here's another. In 2015, there were 372 mass shootings (shootings in which at least four people were killed or wounded) in the United States. These shootings took the lives of 475 people and wounded another 1,870. There are a variety of reasons why each of these murders took place, from passion and metal illness to homophobia to terrorism, and a lot in between.

But besides crimes rooted in passion, mental illness or extremism, consider the description of the typical perpetrator of mass murder. They are usually male and often young. They invariably seem to live mostly solitary lives on the fringes of society. Many, if not most, have mental issues. Last year in Grants Pass, Oregon, just a few hundred miles south of where I live, a young man fitting this description killed nine students at Umpqua Community College. He lived what appears to have been a fairly isolated life in an apartment with his mother. I can't begin to know what his life was like or what led him to do what he did. But clearly, somewhere in his short life, something went wrong. I'm can only assume that during his life, he was exposed to many of the same social interactions that we all experience.

While I can't know how, or if, his life may have been different within a known healthy environment, it doesn't mean that there aren't plenty of reasons to hope a more loving world can only help alleviate this type of desperate behavior. A more loving culture will never make this situation worse.

This is where things are changing. As we march forward to the beat of technology and its correspondingly false sense of meaningful connectedness, there will be people missing the oh-so-important feel of a human touch. This touch could be the tenderness of a hug from a close friend, or an hour well spent talking, in person, with someone they know and trust. But any friendly interaction, whether it's with a friend or a stranger, could have a positive, cumulative effect on the mood and outlook of the people needing it most. Would things have been different in Grants Pass if that same young man had, over the span of his short life, been surrounded by a culture of love and acceptance? Maybe that's exactly what he did receive from his mother and friends. In his case, we will never know.

There are plenty of people who have meaningful relationships via social media and it does provide a valid resource for both healthy and hurting people that they might not get otherwise. But in the case of the ones who are hurting, you will never convince me these people have a realistic chance of getting the help they need by exclusively pleading their case to the Ethernet. Sure there are people listening on the other end. But these other people who may want to actually help, may not even know where the guy lives. He's just another "friend" they talk to once in a while on line.

Consider, instead, the possibility of an alternate outcome if this same hurting person had been part of a circle of friends who met face to face. A close-knit group of loving friends would have had a much better chance of spotting the red flags. Would it work every time? Probably not, but when we see each other's faces and hear the nuances of our spoken words, we are far more likely to pick up on subtle variations in a person's mood. Will the same thing happen in the course of an on-line post? Will someone happen to read between the lines and see trouble, especially when they have to catch up on thirty other posts? Friends, there is no substitute for the loving connections made and nurtured when we are willing to make the effort. Won't you agree, at least in some instances, disaster could have been avoided, lives could have taken a different turn before it was too late? The love we are all capable of sharing can overcome virtually every obstacle. Angry, isolated, brooding people who have given up on the rest of humanity to the point they feel justified in striking out need love's touch more than ever. They won't get it if it isn't offered.

Do you need a reason to believe love can make a difference? For me, senseless violence is a pretty good one. And it's not so much about the fact that actual lives could be saved, as important as that is. It's because the evil in this world is having its way with people who may have given up on the rest of us. Is it possible the world I am suggesting will still have to deal with murder, whether it's one person or twenty? As long as we are on this planet, our human nature will always be on exhibit-good and bad. But pure love given without qualifications or conditions will find its way to the people who need it most. Unless you're an expert at identifying which ones they are, I suggest you love everyone. What's the worse that can happen when we don't? Well... in 2015, it happened 475 times in the U.S.

Another way this senseless mindset is becoming more common is in the latest strategy by terrorists. Since they are being defeated more regularly on the battlefield, they've resorted to doing their best at killing as many innocent people as possible where they live-Paris, London, Barcelona and many other places. Unfortunately they are successful to some extent every time. In the aftermath of each event, two things happen. First there is outrage and sorrow that it happened in the first place. But the second thing that happens is the most important-defiance. Without fail, masses of people stand against the hatred. In many cases, the defiance is demonstrated worldwide. The common theme? Whoever perpetrated the hatred didn't win-no matter what. We, the survivors, link arms in unity and stand in the face of hatred. As one voice, we say love wins, not hate. And this same voice is heard loud and clear whether it's mass murder or a demonstration of racial superiority. Hate loses every time.

It's clear to see this sentiment lives close to the surface in virtually every heart, no matter where we live. It is the singular theme that love never fails and will never be defeated by hatred. This a very good thing, and an even better indicator of what beats in the heart of most people. Love is there and it knows when to come out. Love is in all of us. My hope is that love will be poured out by more of us for the simple reason that it's just a good idea, that it won't always take a tragedy for it come forth. Love can and should be part our reaction to hatred, but couldn't it also become a verb the rest of the time?

I want to convince people we can improve our lives simply by getting acquainted with our best characteristic, the one we all share-Love. As much as I would love to see this take place, it's not going to happen on a worldwide scale. By its very nature, *agape* love is something selflessly starting in one person and being passed on to another. When it's then received and is repeatedly reinforced by the same person or others, it starts to do its work in the recipient. The good deposited in one person eventually reaches a point where it will overflow to others.

The Bible says love is patient. While I would like to see love change our world today, right now, love will always take the time it needs to do its work. Love is irrepressible in its pursuit of us. While our culture clamors for attention, love will always be under the surface waiting to be called upon. Are you willing to allow love to move in you and from you? If you are, this world will be another person closer to becoming an awesome place for all of us.

You are predestined to be a loving person. You are already equipped to dispense love from its inexhaustible resource. It may be deep inside you, but it's there for you when you're ready for it. You are capable of allowing it to make your life more than you ever thought possible and to open your world to the goodness that exists all around you in the people you know and love and in people you have yet to meet. Give love the chance to change your life for the better. When you are willing to do this, we all win. It may take a couple of generations, maybe even longer, but our culture growing in love would be a game changer on a scale none of us could imagine. Don't think for a second that God didn't see this coming. He knew from the beginning that giving us free will would open the door for our best and our worst. This is precisely why he deposited a loving part of himself in each of us. His unconditional love is the only thing able to counteract the disturbing trend our world is following. It's in me, it's in you and it's in every single person you will ever see or meet.

If you need an example of unconditional love, read on. You may be surprised where it comes from. It may even be living in your own house.

1. Relate a story of a time when a stranger did something nice for you.

2. Share your earliest memory of feeling loved.

3. Tell a story of showing a loving kindness to another person (extra points if it was a stranger).

4. Explain why giving at Christmas is different from giving the rest of the year?

5. Has technology improved or hindered our interpersonal relationship

6. Do you agree or disagree with the author's belief that we are naturally inclined to show interest, or at least acknowledge other people?

7. What is the difference between meeting a person at a party and meeting the same person in a less social setting?

8. Do you agree with the author's belief that a more loving culture could alleviate at least some random violence?

9. How is love patient?

10. Do you believe you are predestined to be a loving person?

3
Who Rescued Who?

"Love stinks!"
The J. Geils Band

A few days before Christmas in 2003, we brought our dog, Toby, home from a shelter to become the latest addition to our family. He was only six weeks old and, just like your dog, was the cutest puppy ever. By the time he'd been potty trained and then graduated at the head of the class from obedience school, he'd grown into eighty pounds of muscle, teeth, hair, energy, and love.

Over time, he developed some rather quirky behavior that endeared us to him more every day. He was tall, so he developed the interesting habit of sitting with his hind end on an ottoman and his front paws down on the floor. It actually did look kind of relaxing. From there, he could keep an eye out for squirrels in the front yard. After a while, we didn't pay that much attention to how he sat, whether it was on the ottoman or the floor (or both at the same time). However, when he did finally spot a squirrel, or even sense one, he would start bellowing at the top of his lungs and run to the window to get a better view.

Needless to say, if my family and I were also relaxing in the front room, we would involuntarily jump a couple of feet off the sofa and suddenly have the heart rate of humming birds.

"Toby Batchelor! Knock it off. It's just a dang squirrel." We would yell clutching our chests. He was never easily deterred and would usually whine and anxiously squirm around, switching his gaze between us and the squirrel, who, of course, sat in a tree mocking all of us with that annoying "clucking" sound they make.

At the end of the day, and no matter what he does, Toby owns our hearts. Not once has he ever been very far from me (his alpha). If I'm in a room, he's in there with me. If I go outside, he wants to go with me. Every night he sleeps at the foot of my bed (sometimes on the bed). When we return from a vacation, he runs around the front yard in absolute ecstasy that we've come home yet again. Toby, just like virtually every other pet dog that has ever lived, is the living, breathing embodiment of unconditional love. As far as I'm concerned, our dogs' unique ability to demonstrate love is why God put them here in the first place. Read on. If you don't already agree with me, I think you will. Theirs is a unique existence.

In the first two chapters of this book, I went to great lengths to convince you love is a beautiful thing, it is our supreme emotion. And hopefully, I convinced you that you are a naturally loving creature capable of sharing it with others. Now I'm telling you love stinks (at least The J. Geils Band says it stinks). What gives? Within the right context, like when you're talking about your dog, love really doesn't always smell that great. All dogs can stink at some point. It's part of their job. Have you smelled their breath? Whoa! Of course, if I ate dog food, my breath wouldn't be great either. Many people, including my wife, give their dogs a regular bath, or pay someone to give them a bath. I'm sure there are some dogs that never reach the stinky stage because their owners stay way ahead of it. You know, like those little designer dogs whose feet never touch the ground. Why am I including a chapter about dogs in a book about love? As I stated above, dogs have a unique ability to see through all the clutter and get to the heart of what's important in a relationship. I simply could not leave them out of the love equation.

In spite of their occasional odoriferous condition, we love our dogs, in many instances very deeply. I dare say some of us love our dogs more than we love some people we know, maybe even people we actually love. However, I would never say I love pizza more than our dog, Toby. Come to think of it, Toby, on the other paw, might say he likes pizza better than he likes me. But he rarely gets pizza (even then only the crust) so he may have forgotten.

When it comes to love, dogs blow most masters away in the love department. We, as their masters, love our dogs-we can roll our eyes, smile and turn our face away from their delightfully pungent breath when they get up close and personal or when they leave their hair samples all over the place. But when they ruin a new pair of slippers, we probably don't love them as much. Getting out the shovel to remove the "lawn fudge" before you mow the grass isn't very endearing either.

It's when we react, as humans, to some of the less than favorable things they do, no matter how innocently, that their kind of love for us really shines. They will usually respond by cowering a bit or putting their tail between their legs, but they immediately come to us and say, "Whimper, bark, bark, whine.", which in dog-speak means, "Sorry master, I made a mistake." And even if dogs really could talk, they would never say, "What did you expect Einstein? Hello...I can't operate a shovel without opposable thumbs. You're the one who's supposed to pick up after me! Now get over it and make my dinner!"

No, most dogs only know one way to treat us. That one way is to love us without conditions. Again, I don't think I'm wrong in saying dogs are God's way of showing us what unconditional love looks like. He knew for sure it was a concept we wouldn't necessarily take to naturally. You are a rare and very fortunate individual if a human, of any description, meets you at the front door every day as if you are the best thing they could possibly hope for. I suppose newlyweds get to experience this for a while and even our children are pretty glad to see us when they're a certain age. But I guarantee you, if you got married and one of your wedding presents was a dog, he would outlast your spouse in the I-can't-believe-you-came-home-again category.

So what's my point? Maybe I just happen to like dogs. I guess I've come to realize that the eighty-pound bundle of hair, paws, teeth and muscle we call Toby doesn't act like he loved me any less today than the day we got him. He always wants to be where I am, always by my side like the faithful friend he is.

If you're having trouble with the concept of unconditional love, may I suggest you get a dog? As long as you have a shovel, and take slippers off your Christmas list, what's the worst that can happen? Your new friend will model love for you all day, every day. Someone might ask, "Does it have to be a dog? How about a cat?"-Ahem, let me just say this: Somewhere, in a parallel universe, as we speak, there is a very wise cat writing a book about love. This cat, at this very moment, is suggesting to the other cat readers they get a human so they (the cats, that is) can experience what it feels like to have someone shower them with unconditional love. I saw a good quote once that said; "Dogs have owners, cats have managers." So, to answer your question, "No! A cat isn't the same. Get a Dog!" How about a ferret? No! A turtle? Please.

If I haven't convinced you yet, here's another thing to consider. Having a dog around is sort of like having a "lesser human" to model loving behavior. Although I should point out I have met some dogs who were probably smarter than some humans I've known. Having a dog is similar to finding someone to model love for you all the time without the baggage often associated with having an actual person. But there's a catch: this actual person doesn't really exist, at least when compared to the clutter-free love a dog can demonstrate. This does not mean I don't believe actual people are capable of *agape* love towards other people. If that were the case, I wouldn't be writing this book in the first place. It's just that people have so much other stuff going on in their lives that diffuses the possibility of unfettered, concentrated, unconditional love. Dogs' lives, on the other hand, are not cluttered by much of anything. Besides food, lodging and the occasional romp in an open field, all they really concern themselves with is pleasing their master, and they do this...say it with me, unconditionally.

So, let's say you agree, in principle, that I might be on to something, and you actually go out and purchase a dog. Good for you! I hope it was a rescue animal. Now that you have this living, breathing example of unconditional love living in your house, what's next? My suggestion is you just get to know each other. Let him or her get acquainted with your family and become more comfortable with a new environment. Especially if you now have a rescued animal, there could certainly be some baggage that needs to be addressed on one level or the other. But that aside, let's assume your new family member is pretty normal; take the time to become friends.

Eventually you'll notice Fido really wants to be where you are just about all the time. This will probably be more of an adjustment issue for you than for him, but you'll get used to it. The next thing you may begin to notice is that when you come home at the end of the day, he'll usually be right there waiting to greet you, every day. In time, Fido will continue to demonstrate his devotion in new ways that will endear him to you perhaps like you have never experienced before. These are all very good indications you are both hooked. Now it is worth mentioning that if you get a very young dog, like a puppy, there will be an "adjustment period" that could be kind of challenging. The good news is, especially compared to raising your children, it doesn't last very long. Aside from that first part, (did I mention obedience schools?) you should be able to recognize your life has become a little less stressful than it was before you had your new friend. After all, there's a reason there are organizations taking "comfort dogs" to senior centers, schools and hospitals for the singular purpose of providing a moment of contentment to people needing it most. I recently saw one of the best bumper stickers ever. It was a smallish one that was shaped like a paw print. In the middle, it said, "Who rescued who?" Maybe someone is preempting my idea. By the way, for all you grammar Nazis out there who would say it should be "Who rescued whom?", I already know it's a improper grammar. Duly noted. First, I'm only repeating what someone else came up with. Second, it flows better that way.

Okay so now that you have your shining example of love with you, and everything seems to be going smoothly, how are you supposed to learn from him and apply that to your relationships? I have a few suggestions. First, you may have noticed your dog occasionally smile. That's right, dogs can smile. They basically do it when you would do it, like when they see you after an absence. Just look at their faces and notice their lips and mouth are drawn back into what can best be described as a smile. Now you try it. Easy, huh? The trade: smile when you cross another person's path.

Next interchange, the tail wag. Most dogs seem to be almost constantly wagging their tails. This is one of the basic distinguishing characteristics of dogs compared to their undomesticated cousins. For instance, you probably won't ever see a wolf wag its tail. This may be because they're always hungry and perpetually ready to eat something smaller (or larger) than themselves. The pastor of our church, Pastor Remington, would compare something like this to those emaciated looking supermodels who parade around with a perpetual scowl. It's because they're constantly hungry-they're "hangry". Anyway, back to dogs. How would you wag your tail? If you actually have a tail, you have a whole different set of issues that probably won't be resolved by reading this or any other book, except maybe H.G. Wells' *The Island of Dr. Moreau.* If not, and you're still smiling, you're part way there. If you show genuine happiness when you meet somebody, it's hard for that to be mistaken for something else. When you look someone in the eyes (another thing dogs do), and you have a smile on your face, if you're engaged and interested in the other person, you're figuratively wagging your tail. Obviously you don't want to act giddy or goofy. Just be yourself.

Here's another thing you can do to emulate your canine pal. Dogs love to have their heads rubbed, especially behind the ears. Toby almost goes to sleep standing up when we do this for him. Not surprisingly, the exchange for our purposes does not involve you massaging someone behind the ears. However, if you do, you may have a friend for life. (Do I really need to tell you this is not a good opening strategy on strangers?) What I'm really referring to here is the idea of sharing love as a two-way street. If someone wants to do something nice for you or bless you in some way, let them. If your original goal was to do something nice for someone and in the process, they turn the tables on you, just know this is the way some people show their willingness to receive what you're offering. In some cases, to not receive love in return could weaken or diffuse what you started to do in the first place. Just remember, whenever you set out to be nice to other people, don't be too shocked if they respond in kind. After all, this very thing is our goal, to have a positive, loving exchange between people. If it happens for you, good job! If you feel like it's a one-way exchange, just know you did your part and the return exchange may happen later in someone else's direction. That's okay. You'll eventually receive what someone else planted.

The final interchange I would like to suggest is more general in nature.

Have you ever noticed that dogs are many times the ice breaker for contact between humans? When I was a single man, friends suggested I get a dog because it's a great way to meet women (not that I was having any problems in that department, thank you very much). I never tested the theory, but there's probably some truth to it. There's inherently something about dogs that draws us to them, especially when we're in public. I can't think of a single time during the thirteen years of Toby's life that, while taking him for a walk, at least one person hasn't made a comment about him. Portland, Oregon is a very dog friendly place, so it's more the rule than the exception to see dogs in public. As far as I'm concerned, that, in itself, helps make Portland a pretty nice place to live.

Can you be "the dog" everybody wants to pet when you're out and about going through your day? Of course, it's not that you want to be the center of attention and have people pawing all over you. It's more about your desire to contribute to a friendly demeanor in your own environment. I hope by now, we're on the same page as far as the positive changes possible when we're all working in the same loving direction. Consider the alternative. Do you really want to live in a world of apathy and self-centeredness? Maybe you've noticed our world is heading in that direction. Does any rational person really believe more hatred, or even more apathy, will make this a better world? Dr. Martin Luther King Jr. perhaps said it most astutely when he said, "I have decided to stick with love. Hate is too great a burden to bear." The weight of hatred and disharmony will never be an easy load to carry. Nor will it ever improve anything. You can, for example, see the devastating results of this malignant mindset in the Islamic State. It's so sad to observe the sum of so much hatred and so inconceivable to justify it. Is there a group of people on earth more desperately in need of a demonstration of pure love than ISIS? I doubt it. In fact, I would suggest putting paws on the ground instead of boots. But if you've been brainwashed thoroughly enough, you wouldn't recognize love if it bit you on the ankle. Before we waste another single brain cell on their questionable mindset, let's move on.

Your dog, any dog, whether it's your pet or not, can be a faithful demonstration of what it looks like to love first and ask questions later. Please consider the possibility that love is modeled and demonstrated everywhere on a daily basis by people and dogs. And, yes, there has to be at least one cat out there somewhere that treats somebody with love and empathy. If you're a cat person, sorry for not agreeing with you "unconditionally." That aside, I'm certain we could all learn something about unconditional love if we just spent some time with our canine friends (and that one cat if you can find it). Theirs is a simplified, concentrated version of what could steer us towards a more loving world. I guess the most important thing is that we must open our hearts and minds to the love all around. When we begin to recognize it, we might just discover some open doors we have never even noticed.

When it's all said and done, author J.W. Stephens is probably right when he suggests, "Be the person your dog thinks you are." It's like dogs only see the good in us. If they do detect something that seems bad or they don't understand, they don't care. If we come home and say hello and rub behind their ears, they're good. We can be this kind of person towards people too. The popular phrase, "Wag more, bark less" comes to mind. Can we consider a friendlier approach to others? Actually, having the bumper sticker on your car is probably a good idea. Where else do we humans need to mellow out a bit more than in our cars.

I've said it before and I'll say it again, we choose how to interact with other people. We can choose to have hard edges and ignore the humanity in others, or we can recognize, if we're seeking happiness, hard edges just don't work and never will. If it takes a daily dose of canine love to remind you what this looks like, so be it. Dogs may be man's best friend, but it doesn't mean they have to be your only friend. Maybe if we let our "inner dog" come out more frequently, we'll realize that being an agreeable, open person is a pretty good thing. It doesn't require therapy, good looks or a pile of cash. Start with a smile and the willingness to slow down and live life with other people. Remember, you can't schedule spontaneity. The Bible says a man speaks from the overflow of his heart. So don't be afraid to let people know when you're happy inside. If you're not happy, you can still smile. Who knows, if you get enough smiles back from other people, your mood could turn around. But it has to start somewhere and, just like dogs, people respond much better to wags than barks.

One last thing; I doubt any dog ever wondered about his self image, or whether or not he liked himself. There are some smart dogs out there, but I doubt that even Lassie ever went to a therapist to deal with self-love. We humans, on the other hand, are all capable of falling prey to a less than favorable self image. The next chapter will give you ideas on how you can identify in yourself where you stand on this important issue.

1. How has a pet shown you love?

2. Why can dogs overlook our flaws and love us just the way we are?

3. Why do we seem to struggle to show love the way dogs do?

4. If every single member of ISIS was given a puppy, what do you think would happen?

5. Discuss the quote from J.W. Stephens -"Be the person your dog thinks you are."

6. What do you think it says about a person when they sport a Wag more, bark less bumper sticker?

7. What would our world be like without dogs? (No fair bringing poop into the discussion).

4
Love Yourself First

"The ultimate lesson all of us have to learn is unconditional love, which includes not only others but ourselves as well."
Elisabeth Kübler Ross

For the past fifteen years or so, our family has vacationed on beautiful Lake Shasta in northern California. Typically, we share at least one, and sometimes two, houseboats with friends for the week. To make sure we all get plenty of time to relax, we assign the nightly cooking duties to different families. When it's my family's night, we make a dish called "Steve's Chicken," which is basically grilled chicken with peach infused *pico de gallo*, and some very top-secret sauce. We also make potato salad and green beans. It's nothing fancy, but for some of the people on the trip, this meal is the reason for the trip. I guess it's flattering that people enjoy it so much, but, to me it's not that big of a deal.

Last year, there was a major house-boating emergency, I couldn't go on the trip. Since it's my original recipe and, since I'm the ring leader of our cooking crew, this was a big blow to some of the house-boaters. To appease the masses, my wife volunteered to make the meal sans Steve. I sent her Shasta-bound with very explicit instructions on how to prepare the coveted meal. Reports back from the field after the trip were kind of mixed, but overall the consensus is that while it wasn't exactly the same, it was still pretty good. Even though it had been completely out of my hands, I was kind of disappointed it wasn't just like mine. I knew the list of ingredients had been the same and, well, grilled chicken is grilled chicken. Actually, this wasn't the first time someone else had used my recipe. Two other times, a couple of these same friends (who, by the talking way, are excellent cooks) have made it on their own with similar results; it just wasn't quite the same.

So what happened? I have a theory. Women do things differently than men. I know...who knew? This includes my wife. I don't think I've ever seen her prepare a meal without closely following a recipe as if she's assembling an atom bomb and even the slightest variation could spell nuclear disaster. My wife assembles ingredients days before she's going to make something. I'm not arguing with her style-she's a great cook. It's just different from my style.

Men, on the other hand, generally can't even spell recipe. My wife is incredulous when we have friends coming over for dinner and, two hours before they're due to arrive, I haven't even gone to the store. I tell her I'm going to go shopping and figure something out. This makes her crazy. I know part of the reason why men cook like this, according to anthropologists, is because men "evolved" as hunters. Women are the gatherers. Since I was already there, I agreed to gather also. I guess I kind of agree with this theory since that's pretty much exactly what I do before I cook something. I go over to the grocery store and, with knuckles dragging, grunt around the perimeter gathering stuff that looks good. Does this mean Neanderthal housewives actually had recipes when it was their turn to make dinner? Probably not.

Actually, there are a couple of real reasons why none of the other attempts at Steve's Chicken tasted exactly the same. The first reason is a secret, so if I tell you, you have to promise to keep it to yourself. Okay, I'm whispering now. That recipe I gave them...I left out some of the ingredients. Is that wrong? Maybe, but I did it to protect my exclusive right to make the best dang Steve's Chicken around. What if, let's just say, it's the only thing I happen to have going for me? That's right. Who can blame me?

The other reason is a bit more philosophical. This might have more to do with the disparity in cooking styles between men and women. Again, while many women prefer to "follow the letter of the law" when it comes to recipes, it seems men tend to be more free form, perhaps even serendipitous, when it comes to cooking. When I cook something, even Steve's Chicken, the ingredients will generally be the same every time. But the technique may not be. Maybe I grill the chicken using a different kind of charcoal, or smoke the green beans rather than cooking them in a sauté pan. Sometimes I tweak the ingredients in one direction or the other. For me, that's what makes cooking fun and interesting. Call it artistic license.

At this point, you're probably asking yourself-what can any of this possibly have to do with unconditional love? Have I suddenly decided to turn this into a cookbook instead of a book about love? No, God knows there are already too many cookbooks. On the contrary, we will soldier on with the topic of love.

Let's talk about self-love, a very important topic to cover before we get to the meat of how we hope to render a broader definition of love. Now it would be a huge understatement to say self love has been a well covered subject. In fact, when I Googled self-love, I got a whopping three million, two hundred and forty thousand results! It would take more than the rest of my life to look at each one of those entries. Besides, I'd like to think everything that could possibly have been said about self-love has already been said, (most of it by people who are a lot smarter than I am). I don't expect I could add much of anything to the discussion. However, a few observations are germane to the topic at hand.

Making Steve's Chicken is essentially an analogy for preparing ourselves to share love with others. If it's going to taste right, we must have the right ingredients for what we're trying to do. Think about it. If I'm going to have any hope of being a sincere ambassador of our supreme emotion, shouldn't I make sure I am a qualified source? I am not referring to any professional or formal qualifications, but rather the quality of my own heart. Am I made up of the ingredients that make me love worthy? Earlier in this book I referred to unconditional love as the aquifer from which we draw all loving interaction. What if the aquifer were poisoned or contaminated? That would change things wouldn't it? In the same way, we shouldn't consider ourselves ready to dispense love to someone if we can't first say we at least like ourselves. Again, without adding to the volume of words already spoken about self-love, it should be clear that loving yourself is a necessity for many reasons, but especially if you intend to love outside of yourself. Self-love is the breeding ground of unconditional love. Without it, you're trying to sell something you don't own.

Another way to look at this is to exchange, for a moment, love with respect. Have you ever looked at yourself in the mirror and said something like, "I can't believe I did it again? I am such an idiot! How can I possibly respect myself?" I have just labeled myself as a loser. I know I've had this conversation a few times in my life. And really, I have to say, when I was in the throes of this self-condemnation, the question of whether or not I loved myself never entered my mind. What I did question was whether or not I respected myself. How could I respect someone, including myself, who would do such a thing? The term self-loathing comes to mind. If we go a step further and put self-respect aside, we could insert virtually any emotion and, chances are, we will most likely have placed even more caustic labels on ourselves. Carrying the burden of these self-imposed labels, it's a short stretch to begin labeling other people using the same formula. Consider the following excerpt from C.S. Lewis' *Mere Christianity*:

"For a long time I used to think this a silly, straw-splitting distinction: how could you hate what a man did and not hate the man? But years later it occurred to me that there was one man to whom I had been doing this all my life— namely myself. However much I might dislike my own cowardice or conceit or greed, I went on loving myself. There had never been the slightest difficulty about it. In fact the very reason why I hated these things was that I loved the man. Just because I loved myself, I was sorry to find that I was the sort of man who did those things."

What Lewis so rightly reminds us is that as we go through life measuring others by our own yardstick, we more than likely end up with the same measurement of ourselves. But when we reflect on our own shortcomings, we naturally tend to overlook them because, after all, we are the last bastion of love for ourselves and are, therefore, in most cases, able to forgive ourselves. It is usually far easier to forgive ourselves than to forgive others, yet self-forgiveness is a process taking place every day in both directions. Weigh the alternative; if we didn't forgive ourselves, would we go through life progressively hating ourselves more with every disappointment. It's not like we have some kind of running dialogue with ourselves about what we should or should not forgive; "Okay, you really did it this time! We're finished. I will never forgive you for that one." There are no doubt people having these conversations on a regular basis, sometimes out loud walking down the street. Let's pray they are getting the help they need.

Assuming, as Mr. Lewis states, we become aware it's the action, not the person we dislike, and we are able to apply this distinction to ourselves, we discover we do like ourselves after all. But do we love ourselves? Certainly when we realize we are and have been, as it turns out, forgiving ourselves for as long as we can remember, we really have to say we have, by definition, unconditional love for ourselves. Please understand this is not narcissistic or ego driven. A narcissist is only motivated by love that feeds his unquenchable thirst for self-affirmation and an unrealistic belief in his own perfection. On the other hand, self-love should be a healthy manifestation of what naturally exists in most of us, quietly operating under the surface as a sort of continuous, self-administering litmus test of our emotions.

At the end of the day when we settle our mind and consider events of the past sixteen or so hours, some of us of go through a mental check list of sorts which tells us how we did with our interactions. Does one in particular stand out as disappointing? What could we have done or said differently? If there is something particularly disconcerting, we may dwell on it with umbrage until it is addressed properly. This could be the impetus for making amends the next day with someone or doing something differently in the future. But either way, as far as how we feel about ourselves, it is most likely not going to change us for life. We will move on to the next day of our lives and the process continues. And if we do bring closure to an unsettling issue in a positive way the next day, our decision to not beat ourselves up about it will have been reinforced and justified. When this happens, the system works.

It's easy to draw comparisons to this self-treatment and how we treat others in the same circumstances. With others, we form opinions that can lead to broad conclusions about people that may or may not be fair or warranted. Generally speaking, and assuming we are talking about a fairly normal cross-section of the populace, our human nature tends to produce similar behavior. When one person tears himself down in front of the mirror, somebody, somewhere is probably having the same conversation in front another mirror. Imagine if we all did this every day of our lives. We would have some pretty ticked off people running around. That doesn't sound like much fun. The prospect of this group of stressed out individuals being in the right frame of mind to show unconditional love to each other isn't very good.

Instead, consider the possibilities if each of these people maintained healthy self-respect and didn't dwell on their shortcomings beyond saying they could have done this or that differently. In other words, they didn't carry a self-imposed grudge against themselves into their day. In this scenario, any one of these people could have, for instance, when he noticed a person struggling to load a bulky suitcase into their trunk, offered to help instead of walking on by mumbling to himself about what a loser he is.

So how do we assess our own self-love? I suggest we all give it some honest consideration. Set aside some time to really analyze how you treat yourself and how you honestly feel about yourself.

What has worked for me is to recall how I speak to myself (usually internally, but sometimes out loud), when I do something dumb. Typically, I uses some of my best modified sailor language and move on. It's not always easy, but I try not to let it affect me for very long. Here's a good example. About a year ago, I pulled my beautifully restored 1976 BMW out of the garage and straight into the receiver hitch of our rather large SUV that I had just parked in the driveway. After clearly pointing out to myself that it was one of the dumbest things I had ever done in my entire life, I got on with the business of why I had pulled the car out of the garage in the first place. There was nothing I could have said or done that was going to change anything, so why beat myself up? Even though it eventually cost a thousand dollars to fix my mistake, I didn't suddenly hate myself afterwards. How was I able to recover so quickly? A long time ago I realized I am far from perfect. Therefore, I should plan on screwing something up once in a while. That's what people do. When it happens, I don't let it define me. I vent a bit of steam and move on. Try it the next time you screw up.

Another thing that can help is to discuss how you feel about yourself with your significant other or another close friend. After all, our self-image is something every human has to deal with eventually. If you're talking with someone who knows you well and loves you, chances are that person will give you some positive feedback about yourself that can only help you realize you're worthy of your own love. Sometimes, our self-image boils down to our willingness and ability to believe in ourselves. Even if you have doubts about your own character or you're less than proud of some things from your past, you can still believe you're actually a lovable person. You do have a choice in what you believe. Assuming you have chosen to believe in yourself, you can move forward into developing your self-love into a sort of commodity you can freely dispense. One more thing: as you become more comfortable with showing love to others, don't be surprised when you progressively start to feel better about yourself. It's contagious in both directions.

Read every word you care to about self-love (and there are a lot), but it all boils down to a rational self-image. Consider this, the "Golden Rule" is essentially based on self-love: "Do unto others as you would have them do unto you." The bottom line is maybe we shouldn't take ourselves too seriously. Some of us can be so hard on ourselves, demanding perfection. The fallout of this approach can lead to an unrealistic expectation of everybody else, including our loved ones. This is a recipe for strife and disappointment. Let's be clear, there's nothing wrong with setting realistic expectations for yourself and others, even high expectations. But like everything else, there must be a balance. The balance resides in your ability to love yourself for what you are and use that as a platform to love others. You're not perfect and you never will be. Neither will I. The sooner we all realize this and begin to cut ourselves some slack, the sooner we'll get on with the loving balance this world needs.

Consider the words of John Steinbeck: "And now that you don't have to be perfect, you can be good." This world needs people who are good. I believe you're good or you wouldn't be taking the time to read this book. Can I suggest a quick exercise? Take a few moments and seriously ask yourself: "How do I feel about myself?" Do you respect yourself and really believe you do, or do you have doubts? What might be causing or reinforcing your doubts? Are you starting to believe what others may be saying about you even though you know they're wrong or mistaken?

Perhaps for the first time in your life, forget about what others are telling you about yourself and decide for yourself who you are and who you want to be. Let other people worry about who they are and don't concern yourself with the labels and opinions of others. They can't read your mind any better than they can know what is going on inside your heart. That is your exclusive territory and a picture you alone will paint, a self portrait of your soul. Consider this quote from a famous philosopher:

"Today you are you, that is truer than true. There is no one alive who is youer than you."

Dr. Seuss

You are a unique person and you're created in God's image. He is the author and sovereign creator of all love. If you feel differently, the next chapter may help you understand a different point of view.

1. Discuss with the group why men and women may differ in cooking styles.

2. Describe the ingredients a person should possess to be able to love?

3. Is it possible to love yourself without respecting yourself?

4. Why are we able to look beyond our mistakes and flaws and maintain a healthy self-image?

5. Describe a time you did something regrettable and how you moved past it.

6. How does the "Golden Rule" apply to self-love?

7. How can an unreasonable opinion of yourself affect the way you treat others?

8. Describe how you will determine your own self-image.

5
Love Is God

"God is love. Whoever lives in love,
lives in God, and God in him."
John the Apostle

I never cease to be amazed by the many different ways God can reveal himself to us. The following story tells of one of the most memorable I have ever experienced. In the fall of 1992, the Billy Graham crusade came to Portland. My wife got to be a member of the choir made up of people from our local area. Due to the size of the choir (several hundred), it was not practical for the entire body to practice in one place. Instead, they separated into smaller practice groups and met at area churches prior to the event. The night before the crusade began, the entire choir gathered on the risers at the venue to sing a couple of the songs they'd all been practicing. I accompanied my wife to the stadium in downtown Portland and, while she joined the choir, I sat in the front row of a mostly empty stadium. One of the songs they sang that night was The Lord's Prayer. I believe this is one of the most beautiful songs ever written. Before they were even half way through the song, I had tears streaming down my face as I soaked in the power and majesty of that immense choir as they sang of God's love for all of mankind. It remains to this day as one of the most powerful emotional and spiritual events in my life. I'm certain I got a taste of Heaven that night.

So why did that particular song make such an impression on me? After all, like any other song, it's just words on a piece of paper accompanied by a bunch of squiggly lines and dots. What gave it the ability to transform from letters and symbols into something with the power to birth such emotion? Obviously, there was a gifted composer involved. Albert Malotte, who wrote the music in 1935, had to merge his melody with, in this case, the very words of Christ spoken at the Sermon on the Mount. I suggest this song, just like every other song that glorifies God, is the natural consummation of what happens when God-given talent and genuine love are melded with the resonant truth of God's existence. Whether it's an inspiring musical piece, an exquisite work of art or something as simple as a chance meeting with a new friend, very good things happen when love is the catalyst. And if God is behind it, there is no limit to the magnificence of the outcome.

There are certainly other things that can have a similar emotional reward. One that comes to mind is the beauty and grandeur of nature. We live on a beautiful and diverse planet. There simply aren't words to describe some of what exists in our natural world. Stand on the edge of the Grand Canyon and its awesome beauty and sheer size will take your breath away! If you have ever visited northern California's redwood groves, you were no doubt overwhelmed by the grace and extraordinary dimensions of those magnificent trees. Oregon, my home state, is blessed with a fantastic variety of natural beauty, from its ocean beaches to the Cascade mountain range to the high desert plains. How can you not be awestruck by the world in which we live? For many, it is akin to a near spiritual experience to embrace our natural world.

Or consider the way you feel looking into the eyes of your newborn child resting in your arms. That is love at first sight. The heartfelt flood of emotions in that moment is matchless. When you look into those eyes, it's as if you are looking into the very personification of love itself. Your moistening eyes can't look away from the profound vulnerability and innocence of what is literally a part of yourself. There is an immediate bond forged in those moments that will last a lifetime.

These are just a few examples of our natural world that point to something much larger than ourselves. If you want to experience the majesty of the Grand Canyon, there's only one place you can go-the Grand Canyon. Some things simply have no substitute. You wouldn't go to a public swimming pool and expect to feel anything even remotely close to the way you would feel snorkeling off the Napali coast. The beauty and magnitude of our natural world inspires us like nothing else, and that inspiration can be as unique as the places and people that inspire it.

When I consider the beauty and majesty of our natural world, I see God. I see his incredible creation, the place he created for us. The apostle Paul says, "For since the creation of the world God's invisible qualities-his eternal power and divine nature-have been clearly seen, being understood from what has been made, so that men are without excuse." (Romans 1:20, NIV). Consider how the staggering grandeur, diversity and preeminence of our world has, for century after century, inspired writers, artists and composers to glorify God.

On the other hand, has atheism ever been the inspiration for anything of elegant artistry that will abide as a timeless monument to nothingness? With mankind at its center, atheism has limited itself to what man alone has been able to accomplish. For me, atheism says that beyond our natural organic connection with our planet, we have absolutely nothing in common with the grandeur and magnificence of our world, universe and, ultimately, all that has been, all that is and all that ever will be. This mindset portrays us as very involved observers and stewards with a lot at stake in what we are able to do on our own.

In fairness to atheists and agnostics, being either does not disqualify them from having creative ability that can be the source of beautiful artistic

55

expression. Nor does it keep them from having full, productive lives. I believe they can also experience a form of love, compassion and the many other positive emotions and virtues all humans feel. But I believe there is a permanence associated with love. It is a pure emotion that not only runs like a cord through the length and breadth of human existence, but also continues on through eternity. If you agree that love, our most noble emotion, has always been a part of humanity, I think it would be a mistake to call it just another piece of the flotsam and jetsam of a big bang.

It is love that has been at the heart of our desperate need to prolong our existence on this planet. Love has overcome all of the worst manifestations of our human nature. Love knits the fabric of our families as one and causes us look to the future for the very security and longevity of our descendants. Love will, if you allow it, carry you to a place of comfort for yourself and others. The closer we get to the heart of love's intent, the more the petty concerns of our lives come into perspective. No other emotion can accomplish this.

As much as I'd like to believe that everyone who reads this book has embraced life under the lordship of Jesus Christ, I know that is most likely not the case. If you haven't yet made that spiritual commitment, I hope you will not skip this chapter, or worse, stop reading the book altogether. Please keep this in mind: throughout your life, you have been exposed to many different ideas and beliefs from an abundance of sources and points of view. We are bombarded by information and opinions from every side, much of it born from and motivated by consumerism. I ask you to willingly consider a view not motivated by commerce or any other self-aggrandizing goal. Instead, with an open mind and heart, allow yourself to contemplate a fresh image of what love is and where it came from. In my opinion, love and God are inseparable and, whatever your spiritual beliefs may be, or even if you don't have any at all, when you hear the phrase, "God is Love," you'll understand there is a great deal under the surface of that statement. That simple phrase deserves a deep look.

Maybe you think you've already seen God's love in action in people who profess to be Christians and didn't like what you saw. I've met plenty of people who grew up in the church and either never believed or have since fallen away. Some have gone so far as to have become agnostics or atheists. What can account for such a dramatic turnaround in someone's beliefs? Every person who's walked away from the church has his or her reasons. In my experience, many people I've talked with about their altered beliefs don't attribute the change to a personal spiritual shift coming about after an extended period of self-examination, chronic misgivings or perhaps prayer. Instead, and most unfortunately, the majority have been negatively influenced by the actions of people within the church, maybe a denomination, a church congregation, or even a particular person.

I've attended church most of my adult life and have met people from across the entire spectrum of beliefs, strengths, weaknesses and depths of spirituality. God's church is made up from this collection of qualities. Much the same can be said of society in general. We are a melting pot of beliefs, aspirations and practices. From this melting pot, like-minded people are brought together to experience common interest in sports, the arts, entertainment, politics, etc. It would not be unusual for a person who attends church to also have similar interests they share outside of church.

But it's what prompts us to attend church in particular that is the prevailing difference. While some people attend church to meet spouses, to network, to get free food or as a social obligation, most go to worship God. And we like to do it with other believers. We need and enjoy the fellowship of other people of faith; it strengthens our bonds not only socially, but more importantly, spiritually. We feel communion with God's love as we sing praises to him. We long to hear his wisdom from the pulpit. For myself and others, we want to have a pause in our week, a break from the distractions. Personally, I seek to more profoundly connect with what I believe is the original, inexhaustible source of all love. Many people attend for the same reason.

One thing that has always appealed to me about attending church is that when I'm there, I am comforted and encouraged by the assurance that, generally speaking, I am surrounded by people whose motives I can identify with and trust. And it's not a simple common interest we share, for instance, like members of a model railroading club. My good friend Mike belongs to a railroading club and I have to say, it's very interesting (certainly more for him than for me). But, even for him, model railroading will never fill his soul with unimaginable joy and peace. It's just a hobby and that's all it is or ever should be. There is no human experience comparable with humbly putting yourself in the presence of the living God, especially for the express purpose of telling him you love him and you say yes to him. We attend church, in part, to participate in the permanence of that eternal connection between the author of love and his people.

Therefore, if love has always existed and always will, it has to be a part of eternity past, present, and future. This points to its origin and permanent existence as a part of God himself. I personally can't even begin to understand how our supreme emotion could have somehow begun its existence in an amino acid that somehow arrived on planet earth from who knows where in the cosmos to then evolve into an emotion that would compel a person, and I don't care how many billions of years it may have taken, to look into the eyes of a terminally ill child and wish there were a way they could take her place. Love is not a random mistake that just happened to catch on. Love is what God decided would be the best bonding agent for humanity. He has given us since the beginning of time to accept love for what it is and to treat each other lovingly, with respect and kindness. But even the Father of patience could see we were incapable of making it work on our own. His solution was to come and live among us, to show us what love looks like. The man Jesus Christ was Emmanuel, which means God with us. Of his thirty-three years on earth, only the last three were devoted to his ministry, yet in this short time, he showed us all what love is. His love for us cost him his life. But because he is God, the hatred and ignorance that took his life could not keep him in death. Just as God and his love are eternal, Jesus Christ lives on as well.

The author of love, our eternal God, is the only source of perfected love. If you love, you have a part of God in you. And just as there is a purity in that one emotion, there is a part of his purity in you. When we accept this as truth and embrace a desire for more love in our lives, we have reached the beginning of God. We will, however, never reach the end of God, for he is everlasting.

God has plenty to say about love. In fact, a form of the word love appears seven hundred and seventy-three times in the Bible. Hate, on the other hand, only forty-one. And when hate does appear, it's not in a virtuous light, but rather as an admonishment-as the opposite of love. If you've ever been to a wedding, you have no doubt, heard words of love as they appear in the Bible.

Love is patient
Love is kind
It does not envy
It does not boast
It is not proud
It is not rude
It is not self-seeking
It is not easily angered
It keeps no record of wrongs
Love does not delight in evil but rejoices in truth

It always protects, always trusts, always hopes, always perseveres
Love never fails

I Corinthians 13:4-8, NIV

The apostle Paul was not referring to marriage when he wrote these words, but is there a better definition of what should be the foundation of a loving marriage? Even if they are not spoken in the context of a wedding, these words positively define the perfect model for life and how we should all treat each other. Imagine what this world would be like if every person lived by these words. Read them again; I don't think I'm wrong in saying this. Or consider these other words of Paul the apostle:

If I speak with human eloquence and angelic ecstasy but don't love, I'm nothing but the creaking of a rusty gate.
"If I speak God's Word with power, revealing all his mysteries and making everything plain as day, and if I have faith that says to a mountain, "Jump," and it jumps, but I don't love, I'm nothing.
"If I give everything I own to the poor and even go to the stake to be burned as a martyr, but I don't love, I've gotten nowhere. So, no matter what I say, what I believe, and what I do, I'm bankrupt without love.

I Corinthians 13:1-3 *The Message*

Our world places a great deal of importance on how much we accomplish. The ever-changing measuring stick that can, if we allow it, define our worth is nothing more than another manifestation of our pride as a culture and even as individuals. In this passage, the apostle rightly points out that, regardless of the quality and scale of our efforts, our accomplishments haven't amounted to much of anything if love is not our motive.

As I stated before, what we refer to as the "Golden Rule" is a predominant theme in the Bible - "Love your neighbor as yourself." After spending so much time studying the concept of self-love, I am convinced this rule is a self perpetuating truth. It's like a mirror of love we look into when we show loving kindness to others. Every time we act in love, we reaffirm its value in ourselves.

Without doubt, the ultimate expression of love is revealed in the book of John; "Greater love has no one than this, that he lay down his life for his friends." (John 15:13, NIV). There are countless examples of this throughout human history. Think of the many times a soldier has forfeited his own life to save a brother in arms. Or perhaps you read the recent news story about a young woman in the U.K., Cheryl Anderson, who, along with her husband Leigh, was forced to decide between chemotherapy to treat her cancer, or forego the treatment to save the life of her unborn child. In a great deal of pain, she bravely endured the pregnancy long enough to give birth to their daughter. Sadly, she died later the same day. Sometimes a person is willing to sacrifice his life one day at a time. We've all heard stories about a mother or father willing to put a career or dream on hold so she or he can be there for a growing family. Do you know someone who cares for an aging parent instead of pursuing his or her own life goals?

Ultimately, there can be no condition more sobering than death itself capable of portraying the selfless commitment of unconditional love. The very God of love is not a stranger to a sacrifice of this magnitude.

For God so loved the world that he gave his one and only Son, that whoever believes in him shall not perish but have eternal life.

John 3:16, NIV

Jesus Christ intentionally died an excruciatingly painful death for the sake of mankind. It wasn't a spur-of-the-moment decision. He knew from before the very beginning it would be necessary. Yet even knowing what lay ahead, he still flawlessly demonstrated love with every encounter.

The cord of love God lays down for us to follow never wavers from its ultimate purpose as a pathway to Himself. He has not hidden the reality, power and necessity of love from anyone. People who refuse to see love's cord will continue to trip over it until the very end. Perhaps the wisest thing God has ever done is, in spite of the flawless essence of love that is God himself, he made love a part of us as well. He placed it in our hearts from birth. When we are willing to recognize and embrace him as the originator of what is the best thing about us, we begin a one-way journey to the full knowledge of all love can be. God is love and love leads us to him.

If you believe love is real in your life and not just a random, baseless emotion, then perhaps you have reached the point where you agree something this powerful and good is truly larger than we are and it's the manifestation of God himself. When you embrace this belief, you will begin to experience love on levels you have never imagined. This decision is one you have to make by yourself for yourself. When you agree Jesus Christ is truly God with us and you're willing to confess that genuine truth publicly, you have permanently connected yourself to love's eternal cord.

If God is love and, if therefore, love is God, there is something important for us all to know-God will never do anything evil, or even bad. He only acts in love. There will be times when you may feel God is allowing something to happen that doesn't seem very loving. When it happens, remember God doesn't see things the same way you do. He sees things from an eternal perspective. He already knows where the cord is leading. All he will ever do is what's necessary to keep us as close to the cord as possible. Our job is to act in love as he acts in love. I assure you, he has a lot in store for those who act in love. If you are ready to embrace the best part of yourself and allow it to make a difference in your life and in the lives of others, I say start today, right now. You won't regret it.

God has no problem loving even the most unlovable. We, on the other hand, don't always demonstrate that ability. Regardless, who should we love? How do we decide who should even be on our "love radar"? The next will give you some answers to these important questions.

1. Describe a time you feel can only be described as God's spiritual presence in your life.

2. What are some of the ways God reveals himself to us through our organic world?

3. Describe how love might be defined by an atheist or agnostic.

4. What are some of the things driving people away from the church?

5. Give some reasons why you are or are not compelled to attend church.

6. During his time on earth, how did Christ demonstrate how love is supposed to work?

7. Describe an instance of selfless love shown by one person for another.

8. Describe how God's eternal cord of love has touched your life.

6

Premeditated Love

"Who do you love?"
George Thorogood and The Destroyers

Believe it or not, you can learn to love anyone. Much of your ability to love lies in your willingness to look at people from a different point of view.

Every year, the church I attend serves Christmas dinner at a downtown mission that focuses on caring for the homeless. In addition, we pass out backpacks with some essential supplies for life on the street. The people who come in to be served typically represent a similar cross section of the people who aren't homeless-in other words, people like you and me. Some are the career homeless who don't seem to be able to break the cycle. Others appear to be new to it and don't yet show the ravages of what is a very difficult existence. A few even have young children with them. A friend who worked last Christmas related a story that not only illustrates the challenges some of the homeless face, but the issues that arise when we love them through service.

At this particular meal, there was an elderly woman who was, well, let's say she was eccentric. She was bundled up in a mish-mash of coats, scarves and other random layers of clothing. Our friend noticed, beyond the woman's ensemble, she could see what appeared to be the face of a cat tightly swaddled in the folds of cloth. If the cat's eyes hadn't been moving around, she might have thought the woman was carrying a cat's head inside her coat. Sitting near this woman was a young couple with an infant. The eccentric woman seemed very interested in the child and eventually made a couple of short visits to see the baby up close. On her third visit, she said, "Your baby is darling. I'll trade my cat for the child."

The mother, who was holding the baby at the time, held her child closer and glared. Her husband smiled and said, "Oh thanks, but I think we'll keep the baby." Even though he was a young man, even his limited experience of living on the road had taught him to take things with a grain of salt.

The woman seemed surprised. "Are you sure? She's a very nice cat."

Still smiling, the young man said, "I'm sure she is. We like cats too, but I think it would be best for us to keep our daughter."

"Well...okay, but if you change your mind, I'll be right over here." The woman frowned as she walked back to her seat.

As this story clearly illustrates, some of the homeless have challenges with their mental health. But many just need a good meal and the opportunity to catch up on their personal hygiene. And regardless of where any of them fall on the "lovable" scale, the volunteers from our church do not treat any one of them differently from the next. The choice to love them all had already been made when they volunteered.

Obviously, if someone volunteers to serve a meal and share kindness and a smile with the homeless at an event scheduled months in advance, there's not much spontaneity involved. This naturally begs the question. If any of these volunteers had been just walking down the street and encountered the same homeless people under different circumstances, would they have acted differently? Would they have even been paying enough attention to notice the same person if they were huddled in a doorway trying to keep warm? The answer is more than likely, no. And it's not that they have turned off their compassion radar or they no longer care. What's happening is they are, at that moment, going through the paces of their life. Most of us are not constantly looking for opportunities to show love or compassion to every person, homeless or not, we encounter in our day.

This is not a bad thing. It's just the way people live their lives. In the same way, the person huddled in the doorway is in the midst of living his or her life. Now at any point in this conversation, a reader might assume both of these people have chosen the life they're living. Therefore, how could we expect the non-homeless person to acknowledge and care for every homeless person he encounters? Clearly, the homeless have chosen to be homeless, right? Why else would anybody live like that?

Let me just say this: First of all, this is not an uncommon point of view, but with very, very few exceptions, it is also not a fair statement to make. Think about it; why would anybody choose to live like that? Most clear-thinking people wouldn't. Most of the people who end up on our streets are there because of some poor choices or because something in their lives went south and they weren't fortunate enough to have either the resources or know-how to get themselves back on track. It doesn't mean they want to stay there. We will look more deeply into this issue later. For now, let's make the assumption that we will all be presented with a multitude of different physical, emotional, and even spiritual situations that could include virtually every description of humanity whether they're living in a mansion or a cardboard box. The question this chapter asks is who do we love? Who will be the beneficiaries of our "love largesse"? We will get into the how part in a later chapter.

So, who do we love? Maybe not surprisingly, I say we should love everybody. I can almost hear some readers saying, "Man this guy is a simpleton. Is it really possible to love everybody?" They might be right (about the simpleton part). But love should be simple. If it isn't, we're overthinking it. *Agape* love is pure, uninhibited, unconditional love. The love that's always dressed in the perfect outfit for every occasion. We can bring it anywhere.

The reason I say we should be ready and willing to love anyone is because if we're not, then we're attaching conditions to our love. This would work if we were at a pizza buffet: "I like that, but I don't like that and, oh that looks good and, wait, who puts carrots on a pizza?" It's okay to judge pizza. But with people, especially people who really need to feel a loving connection, we don't have the luxury of pre-qualification. If the loving culture I believe could change our world is going to function, it can't be discriminatory.

We will invariably cross paths with people who are in need of some loving attention. What if it's not all that obvious? Our culture has conditioned us to at least give the appearance we're always in control of our lives and emotions. We don't want anyone to know, or even suspect, we may be hurting inside.

Dr. Leon F. Seltzer, writing in *Psychology Today*, points out: "Tendencies toward denial, withdrawal, and self-isolation are common in reaction to deeply felt emotional pain. In fact, one clue that a person is feeling distressed may be in their becoming unusually quiet or shut down. Such silence speaks volumes, and generally the message is: 'I'm not going to risk your hurting me more than you already have...so I'm putting a wall between us.'" When you see a person who appears to be quiet or withdrawn, you have to be aware they truly could be hurting inside. Did you bring the hurt causing them to withdraw? If so, both of you have some work to do. If not, you must be willing to understand their need for positive input. Hearing and receiving something positive from anybody can only help, and it is precisely this hurting person who needs what we have to offer. That being said, and this is key, is there any chance at all this person will feel love, understanding or compassion if the rest of us are going through life emotionally disconnected from the rest of society? It's doubtful. We will certainly encounter hurting people in our lives. It's when we take off the blinders and have our eyes, and our hearts, open to what, or should I say who, is happening around us, we will start to become part of the solution to the emotional apathy surrounding our lives.

Here's another way to look at it. Ana Swanson, a reporter for Wonkblog, states in an article published by The Washington Post, that, according to the Pew Research Center's annual Global Attitudes survey, 48,643 respondents, from a cross-section of 44 different countries worldwide, were asked a friendly first question as a way to relax them towards the interviewer. They were simply asked how their day was going. The global median was 65% having a typical day, 27% having a good day, and 7% having a bad day. Somewhat surprisingly, the study showed 41% in the U.S. were having a good day with only 8% having a bad one.

Therefore, speaking in terms of the United States (in 2014), how would this break down for our purposes? The population of the United States at the beginning of 2014 was estimated to be approximately 318 million people. Given that number, and assuming, as this research suggests, 8% of them were having a bad day, we can therefore loosely estimate there were just over 25 million not having a good day. In fact, they would have called it a bad day (I hope they weren't all in the same place). So, from this estimate, we can assume one in twelve people could probably use a hug, or at least a smile. I would call that a target-rich environment. Going a step further, let's say you're working in an office with twenty-four other people. This means at least two of those people are having a bad day. The thing is, they may not be demonstrating some abnormal (for them) type of behavior, so you won't know who they are. Now suppose you have recently made the decision to take my advice to heart and reach out to people. Plus, you know, based on my very unofficial estimate, there must be a couple of people in your office who, at the very least, could use a smile, and probably more. Do you subtly ask leading questions? Do you tell a couple of jokes and notice who doesn't laugh? The answer to either question is no (especially if you can't tell a joke).

If you presume, going in, that there are at least two people, statistically speaking, who aren't having a good day, who should you love? Obviously these two should already be on your list. But this is assuming you know who they are. Instead, just love everyone in your office. We're keeping it simple, right? You show the same level of interest and openness to the whole group. Please don't think I am trying to turn anybody into some kind of personal therapist or glad hand to the masses. I'm merely suggesting that if you were to open yourself to your co-workers, you could open the door for deeper relationships that could surely benefit the climate of your work space. Your only ulterior motive is to soften life around the edges. What if it turns out there is someone you already know who would really like to talk about a troubling aspect of his life? Or it could be something much simpler. Maybe there's someone new in town who hasn't felt welcome yet. You want simpler? Maybe there's a guy who's just having a bad day and could use some help changing the subject. Your simple smile could be all it takes to turn his day around. If they need more, a smile is still a good place to start. Ignoring them all day certainly isn't going to help. At this point, some might say it's none of your business if a co-worker is having a problem. You already have enough on your own plate. Would the person saying this please go back and start reading this book over from the beginning? You're entirely missing the point.

Leaving the naysayers aside, imagine working in a place where everybody treated each other with love and compassion. For me, it sounds like a pretty nice place to work. Maybe, just maybe, it would eliminate office politics. Is it possible work could get done more efficiently, productivity could increase? Who knows, maybe you'll get a big fat raise! Whoa, whoa, whoa, pardner...time for a reality check. You're right, let's not get carried away. Suffice it to say, and I hope you agree, genuinely opening ourselves to each other consistently, without an agenda beyond creating a friendlier coexistence, can only improve any situation whether it's at work or in our personal lives. This is especially true if your current situation is unfriendly. Conversely, if you already work in a friendly, cohesive place and genuinely look forward to being there, congratulations. But I assure you, even in that environment, there are still people who, given the chance, would probably welcome having someone they could turn to occasionally. Remember, even if we are, essentially, working with friends and everybody seems to be doing quite well, we are all capable of masking a troubling issue. So instead of becoming experts at disguising the emotions that are bottled up inside, let's approach our interactions from a different point of view, one that will allow for some transparency and openness. I'm describing an environment with a culture of caring and involvement as opposed to one that keeps everyone emotionally isolated. Regardless of your situation at work, this approach is something everyone might need to practice. But if there's any chance it could nurture a more loving environment, why wouldn't we give it a try? If you are trying to earn a living in a place characterized by an undertow of mistrust, bickering and dysfunction, wouldn't you be open to something that might not only improve the situation, but perhaps turn it around completely? And, while nurturing a good-natured and engaged work environment should be near the top of every manager's skill set and job description, many companies haven't made the connection between a peaceful, respectful and friendly work place and how essential it is to the bottom line. This is where you come in. You can make the choice to nurture a loving and supportive work environment. It can and does happen sometimes with the smallest things, like saying good morning with a smile.

Before this starts looking like a how-to manual for the dysfunctional work place, I'll remind you the same principles apply at home, school or wherever people gather. The way you treat other people, regardless of the setting or situation, really should not be dramatically different from one environment to the next. A smile is a smile whether it's towards the guy in the mail room or the bus driver on your way home. Remember you're not limited to a prescribed number of smiles every day. And I'll bet you could say, "How was your day?" to anyone as many times as you like.

Who should we love? Again, I see everyone as a candidate. Personally, I sometimes go out of my way to proactively be an open and loving person. For example, if I am in a certain setting and I see someone who, either by his demeanor or his attire, looks a bit out of place, I'll make sure I acknowledge him and try to engage him in friendly conversation. This is related to what I said earlier about my reluctance to ignore someone when I'm close by. I feel even more compelled to make someone feel welcome and accepted when they appear to be ill at ease. If you've ever been to Portland, you've probably heard the term "Keep Portland Weird," because every other car has it as a bumper sticker. There are even some clever variations on the theme like, "Keep Portland Wired," put out by a local electricians' union and "Keep Portland Beered" from people who, well, must really like beer. I've recently heard that Austin, Texas is attempting to get in on the "weird" band wagon. Posers. Actually, someone told me recently that it started in Austin. I say, prove it.

Portland does have a rather large weird faction and no shortage of interesting looking people. I think I'm the only guy who doesn't sport a tattoo. People actually give me weird looks because of it. So with Portland's disproportional population of provocative-looking people, it's inevitable the fascinating will cross paths with the not-so-fascinating. Sometimes, these traditionals have been known to actually stare at the fascinating. I think that's rude and misinformed. Why does a person decide he will have gauges the size of golf balls in his ear lobes? Only he knows. It doesn't keep me from making it a point to engage with him in a friendly way. If anything, I think I have kind caught some of these people off guard. I am a fairly conservative-looking guy in his early sixties. That I would even not stare is a bit surprising to some of them. That I would actually strike up a conversation is invariably a little disconcerting. But with very few exceptions, these people relax fairly quickly when they realize I'm not being patronizing or trying to make fun of them, but, rather, just showing friendly interest. Except for the way some of them look, most are very normal people with normal lives. It's kind of funny to notice when I've started having a conversation with one of our interesting residents, the person who started out staring at them, switches their gaze to me.

The lesson? Don't judge a book by its cover. There's no shortage of interesting people in this world, and just because they may not fit your definition of normal, doesn't disqualify them from the need to be acknowledged and engaged. It should go without saying that everything I just said applies equally to people who are of a different race from our own, or embrace a different sexual orientation. Regardless of the color of our skin, the quantity, size, and location of our tattoos, or the way we put on our pants in the morning, we are all here with the same hope of being accepted for who we are and being allowed the right to live in peace. If you come across anyone of the people who fit this description, which I hope by now you have gathered, means anybody and everybody, it is your right, your privilege and your job as a fellow member of the human race to acknowledge them as people who just want to be accepted and loved for who we all are-children of the living God.

One group most in need of a smile are the homeless. We talked briefly about this earlier. Unfortunately, the homeless are also one of the most ignored members of our society and, at the same time, the ones most in need of friendly recognition. Ask any of these people what bothers them most about their lives and they'll probably tell you they feel as if they are invisible. Many homeless people are on the street because something in their lives didn't work out the way they'd planned and they're having trouble recovering from it. But many have emotional issues that they self-medicate with drugs and alcohol. This doesn't mean they're all drug addicts or alcoholics, nor are they all lazy. Clearly they have had some issues, but unless you actually know what brought them where they are, it's a mistake to always assume the worst.

Consider the following scenario: in Portland the average two bedroom apartment rents for about $1300 per month. Presumably, a nice one costs far more. Let's also say you are married and have two children. You work at a minimum-wage job, which around here is a whopping $9.75 an hour. If you work 160 hours a month, your gross income is $1560 a month. But you'd only bring home around $1100 every month. This means, after taxes, you start every month $200 short on your rent. Oh, you want to eat? Well that's another $400 and, what, you have to buy gas so you can drive to work or buy a transit pass? You can see where I'm going with this.

Given this all too common scenario, it isn't hard to see how people can end up on the street. Are there social services that can help subsidize people in this situation? Of course. And obviously drug and alcohol abuse can exacerbate the problem. But assuming a good portion of our homeless have innocently ended up in a tough situation, perhaps we should be willing to admit that by the grace of God, we have been able to avoid the same fate.

I understand the dynamic of how we interact with the homeless. If we do acknowledge them, we feel like we're opening the door for them to ask for money. That is certainly a possibility, but you can always say no. All I have read about this issue says it is a mistake to give money to someone on the street. If they're being honest, homeless people will tell you the same thing. Okay, but that doesn't mean they should be ignored. I have talked with many homeless people who tell me they can always get a decent meal at a number of different resources in our city. Many are also able to find shelter available and there are some who choose to stay put where they are. Life on the street is a unique world most of us will never experience or understand. If you have the time, ask them how they're doing and, if you feel it's appropriate, offer them some help. But please don't treat them as if they don't matter. Perhaps if we started treating the homeless like valid members of our world, they would start to act the part. Could this transformation start with a simple smile? We won't know until we try.

One last suggestion regarding the homeless is to spend some time around them under different circumstances. It's pretty easy to do this by volunteering at one of the places they frequent, such as missions or care centers. These non-profits will always welcome hands-on help. By doing this, you will get a glimpse into the lives of people who live under far different conditions than yourself. Spend some time around them, and I'll bet you'll look at them differently. One thing you'll realize is that most of the people who show up for a decent meal or a new pair of socks are pretty normal. You may even discover some of them, especially the younger ones, seem embarrassed to have their hands out. Another thing you'll find is they're grateful. These are the people who populate the recesses of our world. Get to know them even a little bit, and a couple of things should happen. First, you'll realize they're mostly pretty decent people. Second, you'll grasp that compared to the average homeless person, your life, by almost any definition, is not too bad. If you have children, bring them with you to help serve a meal. When you get home, talk together about what it means to share your time and resources with people less fortunate than yourselves. But most importantly, make sure your kids understand these people aren't aliens to fear and ignore, but human beings who deserve our love as much as the next person.

There is another part of our humanity that deserves mention as well. You may have noticed them from time to time. Some of them like to sit on park benches and feed the birds, they move a little slower than we do and, among other things, most of them have gray hair. You know who I'm talking about-they're you in the future. That's right. Our seniors weren't imported from another planet just to drive around with their left turn signals on and eat dinner at four o'clock in the afternoon. In fact, if you're fortunate enough, you will become a senior citizen some day. Thanks to medical advances, more people are living longer, which means there will be more elders than ever before. I heard the other day that sixty is the new forty. I assume they were talking about age not speed limit.

Some elders are doing quite well and still have sharp minds, fit bodies and full, independent lives. But many haven't aged quite so gracefully and have both physical and mental health issues that are sometimes compounded by challenging financial situations. These fellow citizens deserve not only our love, but our respect. When you are respectful and loving by doing something as simple as helping them with their grocery cart or holding the door for them, they are usually grateful. Most of them come from a generation where young people were raised to be respectful of their elders. That admirable aspect of our culture needs to make a comeback. It's worth remembering many seniors are part of what author Tom Brokaw accurately calls The Greatest Generation. They stepped up, defeated evil with their blood, sweat and tears, then got on with life raising families and paying taxes.

This is a natural segue to the next population group who should never be overlooked – our veterans and active duty military. Again, there were thousands of men and women who not only performed military service during World War II, but worked long shifts in shipyards and factories. Our World War II veterans are dying at a rate of almost five hundred a day. Before long, they won't be around for us to thank. There are vets from Korea, Vietnam, the Gulf War, Afghanistan and Iraq. We owe them all a debt of gratitude and respect regardless of how we feel about war. They were willing to put their lives on the line and, as stated earlier, that is the ultimate show of love for another.

As for our active-duty men and women, not only are they putting their lives at risk, they are living through long periods of separation from loved ones in far off places where they aren't usually embraced as friends. When they do come home, the last thing that should happen to them is to be ignored or, even worse, disrespected. They are all willing to do something many of us don't have the courage or the will to do ourselves.

Personally, I consider it a privilege to shake the hand of a person in uniform or a war veteran and tell them thanks for what they're doing or what they may have done whether it was in 1942, 1953, 1967, 1991 or 2016. Most of us will never know what it's like to do something as simple as eating an MRE in a stateside field exercise, not to mention ever experiencing the horror of actual combat. Many of our active military and veterans have war-time memories that are permanently etched in their minds no matter how long ago they occurred. When you say thanks, for some of them, it's still so fresh, it's as though you said thanks for service that just ended. I urge you to make it a practice of saying something as simple as "Thanks for serving" to the next veteran or active military you see. Trust me, it'll mean a lot. I know it does when someone says it to me. And while we're on the subject of saying thanks, regardless of what pictures are painted on the nightly news, saying thanks to police officers qualifies as well. They put their lives on the line every single time they put on that uniform. I appreciate what they do to keep our society safe. I hope you do too.

There are a few more groups of individuals I want to make sure aren't bypassed as we consider who we should love. First are children, and I mean our own children of course, but all the other ones too. It goes without saying our children are growing up in a dangerous world. Activities I took part in when I was a child growing up in the fifties and sixties would probably be called child endangerment today, like playing hide and seek well after dark and only coming home when our mom or dad called us from the front porch. Even when my sisters and I were young, our parents taught us to be careful about speaking to strangers. If anything, it's even more important to be careful now. We all understand the significance of the term stranger danger.

In spite of what this world has become for our young ones, I believe we can nurture a friendly environment within the framework of safety and common sense. Most kids are naturally inquisitive about the world around them. We've all sat in a restaurant and noticed a little kid staring at us from a nearby table. Instead of ignoring them, why not smile and wave? They're still safely ensconced within the confines of their family unit and we have shown them a friendly face. Clearly, there are some very well-defined boundaries that must be respected whenever there are children involved. But remember, we're trying to open ourselves to others. When we acknowledge the presence of a young family who happen to cross our path, don't leave their kids out of the occasion.

I recently attended a soccer game and struck up a conversation with a precocious five-year-old boy who was sitting nearby, next to his dad. He was a real character and I thoroughly enjoyed myself. That little boy knew he was able to have some fun with a guy he didn't know because his dad accepted me. It's very important to respect those boundaries and always follow the lead of the parent. You might be thinking I'm on pretty thin ice by even suggesting any type of interaction with a child under any circumstances, whether the child's parent is there or not. Believe me, I agree with that point of view. However, to me it feels like every day, our society gets a little closer to us all becoming permanent strangers with no mechanism in place that gives us the chance of living together in peaceful coexistence. The way that is going to change is through our thoughtful, genuine openness to each other. Our children, when treated in a friendly, uncompromising and respectful manner by other people might learn some good habits that could carry on throughout their lives. On the other hand, if our children see us treating each other with apathy and mistrust, they will learn to be the same way we are. Don't we have a choice in what we will perpetuate?

Our next group of people are perhaps the most vulnerable. These are the people among us with physical or learning disabilities. I'm not sure I can think of anything more disturbing than witnessing someone having a laugh at the expense of a disabled person. This is ignorance, stupidity and arrogance on a monumental scale and will never be acceptable. The healthy young man blessed with good looks and exceptional physical attributes had no more choice in how he would be born than the kid born with Tourette's Syndrome, or any other challenging condition. Therefore, he has no right to do anything more than be thankful for the traits he was born with. I know a young man who was born with good looks and above average physical abilities. Instead of using his traits as weapons, he goes out of his way to make less fortunate people feel welcome and respected. This man is my younger son. I would like to think he got this all from me and my wife, but I'm convinced there is a place in his heart that allows him to see the inadequacies of others as something to be embraced rather than mocked. I could make the same statement about my daughter and eldest son. Every time any of us goes out of our way to acknowledge a challenged person, we are building them up. We are telling them they matter.

The next group of people may be the most challenging to love. Most of us are around them for at least part of our day, but we rarely have a reason to interact or talk with them directly. The dynamics of loving this group come with a whole different set of requirements not part of the picture with any other group. The people I'm referring to are other drivers. Theoretically, the way we act when we drive should be a microcosm of how we interact with people outside our cars. But when we're driving, there is something happening to many of us that runs counter to normal behavior. We all know someone we like and admire who is very pleasant to be around under normal circumstances. However, put this person behind the wheel and they go through a transformation. They exhibit the capacity to go from lovable to unlovable in an instant. This person might even be you. I have driven for a long time and this phenomenon seems to have gotten worse over the last several years. I put most of this change at the ever quickening pace of life. When combined with a self-centered sense of entitlement, we have the recipe for an all-out war on the highways. The worst embodiment of this is road rage. It really is an ugly term. If you've ever been involved with it, you know how disconcerting it is to your emotional state, not to mention the danger involved. Even if you just witness it happening between other drivers, it's disturbing. But while road rage has unfortunately become more common, it is an exception to the typical behavior that exists between normal drivers.

Why is it we can behave so differently when we get behind the wheel?

I believe it has a lot to do with the sense of security we feel when we are within the confines of our vehicle. Is a person driving a big SUV more likely to drive with a sense of domination than a person driving a Smart car? How about the guy in a new BMW compared to the one in a worn out 1978 Corolla? I do believe a hierarchy of sorts exists on our highways, but what we drive doesn't make us a better driver any more than playing a brand-new Fender Stratocaster instead of a beat up acoustic with three strings missing make us a better guitar player. You can either do it well or you can't. A good guitar player could make a three sting guitar sound pretty good. The difference is ability and desire. If you're a bad or discourteous driver, for a whole lot of reasons, you can and should try to get better at it.

Why should we extend love to other drivers? For the same reasons we should extend it to anyone; it just makes the world a more pleasant place. And in this case, a safer place. If we intentionally look for opportunities to be congenial towards other drivers, we take some of the stress out of the driving experience. In the next chapter we will talk about how to go about being loving drivers, but, for now, I hope you'll agree if we're going to be more loving in our interpersonal, day to day lives, it sounds kind of crazy to turn it off once we get behind the wheel of our cars.

The next to last group I will consider are the people who may or may not agree with my political point of view. Our recent presidential election brought this disparity into focus like never before. This could be people who are running for office or their supporters. I was quite surprised at how polarizing this became. It reminded me of the Civil War, when brothers fought brothers. Even in my church, people not only chose sides, but were quite outspoken about their view point. It was as if any sense of reason or openness had flown out the window. Now that the election is over, much of the vitriol has gone by the wayside. But it was tough for a while. How did I get through it? I looked farther down the road. I knew it would eventually settle down and what had the potential to be divisive, would simmer down.

What if the same thing happens during the next election? Hopefully I will have had four years of being a loving person to keep me in a more stable emotional state. I can go into it with a loving perspective that will help me keep my soap box and boxing gloves in the closet (where they've always been). There's nothing wrong with having an opinion that others may not share. But when that discussion buries the whole reason we're here in the first place, to treat each other with love and respect, it's gone too far.

The final type of people who deserve to be set apart for special consideration are probably the dearest people in our lives; our families. Maybe you don't think this is worth mentioning, since these people are our "loved ones." Most of us would say we already love our families. Why, and how, should I love them more than I already do? Both are valid questions. But in this case, I am referring to love in a different context. As we discussed earlier, the love you have for your family is referred to as *storge* (stor-gay) love. This type of love is unique to your immediate family and if yours is genuine and healthy, then you have a great foundation for continued success. But for a moment think about the day-to-day interactions among these very same family members we love with a special kind of love. Are our interactions always loving? If you are like most normal families, including my own, they probably aren't.

Now I may be one of the nicest guys you'll never meet, but sometimes I'm not the most loving person. I can say the same thing about the rest of my family members, and they would agree. There are times when I can talk with complete strangers more courteously than I do with my own wife, whom I love dearly. I am most assuredly not alone in this type of behavior. And I'll wager you can remember a time when someone was describing how sweet and polite one of your children was and, while you nod in agreement, you're thinking they must must have been referring to some child you didn't even know you had. They couldn't be talking about your kid. Fortunately, even our own children often reserve their worst behavior for the special people in their lives.

There's been much discussion about why this happens, and I've made it clear I am not equipped to explain the many underlying reasons we do what we do. From what I've been able to determine, a great deal of this type of behavior is born from angst or even traumatic experiences left over from our childhood. In many cases, those experiences can contribute to a poor self-image. Sometimes, within the security of genuine loving relationships, and especially when combined with our own inability to love ourselves, these experiences can resurface as self-doubt and even self-loathing. Given the right set of circumstances, they can bubble over into our most precious relationships. To me, especially when I think of the times I've been a knucklehead to my family, this makes sense. Can I figure out what may have happened in my early years that contributes to this type of behavior? Probably not without the help of a professional. For me, just knowing I'm capable of not always acting in love towards my loved ones is enough for me to be careful about my words and actions.

In an earlier chapter, we talked about the need to have a positive self-image, to actually realize we love ourselves. I don't believe most of us will require months of psychoanalysis to learn how to love ourselves. But I do believe when we intentionally act in love towards other people, it will reveal something within ourselves that can best be defined as self-love. When this takes place, it should naturally allow us to treat everyone, and especially our loved ones, with respect and with love. If you realize and are willing to admit you seem to strike out emotionally at your family, it might be time to stop and do some self examination. If you need help doing this, get it. There are people in your life who depend on your love. Showing respectful, consistent love to your family is not unnatural and shouldn't be unusual, but it's not always automatic.

In order for us to rule out the possibility that we may be hindered by a lack of self-love, we must determine where we stand. Have a frank, but loving conversation with your family about any doubts you may have about your self-image. Talk honestly with your loved ones and get their take on it. But when you do, be prepared to hear some things you might not like. They may have to be prepared to do the same. If there are some troubling aspects of your self-image and you can get them out on the table and confront them honestly, your family life could become something it hasn't been for a long time, or maybe never was. The bottom line is that these particular people deserve your very best attempt at unconditional love all the time. I don't think any of them would mind if you practiced on them.

No one should be exempt from our open, friendly, and loving attention. To be willing to treat others this way will no doubt be a stretch for some people. To then actually do it will be an even bigger stretch. I'm sure you have figured out it is not a stretch for me to open up to people. It is a part of my personality that I can't really explain. But what I do know is every time I have even the slightest positive interaction with someone, and this is especially true with strangers, I feel like my life gets a little bigger, a little fuller and the world in which I live isn't quite so harsh. In the following chapter, we will discuss some strategies for implementing and expanding our loving influence on others. But for now, who do you love? Love everybody, but especially the precious ones right in front of you.

1. Describe a time you showed unconditional love to a stranger.

2. Describe a positive interaction with a homeless person.

3. What are some of the ways we attach conditions to showing love?

4. Why do we want other people to believe we're always emotionally stable?

5. How could a loving environment improve the workplace?

6. Describe a time you met someone who seemed "different," but who turned out to be quite normal.

7. Why should we show love and respect to elders, members of the armed service and children in particular?

8. Why should we be loving and respectful to the disabled?

9. Why is driving such a challenge when we are trying show love and respect?

10. Why is the dynamic for unconditional love different with our immediate family members than with strangers?

11. Who should we love and why?

7
How Do We Love?

"Don't look for love. Quietly give it away and let it find you back."
Anonymous

A couple of weeks ago, I attended a memorial service for a friend named Barbara. This sweet woman had three daughters and a number of grandchildren, all of whom were at the service along with her three sons-in-law, extended family and a few hundred friends. Like any service of this type, sorrow and grief were unmistakably plain to see, but they weren't the theme. The theme had more to do with Barbara's character as a mother, grandmother and friend. The word garden came up a lot. She loved to garden and spent hours caring for her flowers, plants and vegetables.

Barbara's interest in gardening carried over into the rest of her life even more profoundly. For her, everyone dear in her life was cared for as if they were beautiful flowers growing in her personal garden, her "love garden." The fruit this garden produced was plain to see in the lives of her children, grandchildren and family. You might say she transplanted healthy plants into their own lives. She nurtured them with love and attention. When she met a new friend, her radiant smile made them feel welcome.

In her life devoted to tending living, growing things, Barbara learned early on that, to be successful as a gardener, requires more than part-time effort. She knew for plants to thrive and be fruitful, consistent care would be essential. It was a choice she made for her garden, but more importantly, a choice she made towards her loved ones. It was as if she'd decided, I love these people. Therefore I will watch them grow and I'll never miss an opportunity to help them be stronger, more beautiful and loved. Her last act on earth was to make cookies for her grandchildren. As they were cooling on the kitchen counter, she lay down on the sofa to rest. That's where she was found hours later, to the very end, tending her love garden.

During the service, the pastor referred to, Jeremiah 31:12, NIV. "They will be like a well-watered garden, and they will sorrow no more." This well-chosen verse describes how Barbara approached the life of her family. When she passed on, she didn't leave behind a desert. On the contrary, Barbara left a fruitful garden thriving in rich, well-watered soil filled with beauty and hope.

As we move forward into the how of loving others, it's important to remember that love only comes to fruition when it is given away. As my friend Barbara learned a long time ago, love only grows when it's nurtured. Expecting otherwise would be like expecting a garden to grow without ever putting seeds in the ground. That must take place before anything else will happen. When the seeds are in the ground, the sower becomes the caretaker, the gardener. Only then can he have anything to enjoy, to give away. So if you agree that I might just be on to something, if you believe you are, or can be, a loving person confident in your ability to demonstrate it freely, if you believe you really could make a difference, then it's time to put your belief into practice.

What we're about to undertake should never be thought of as a singular task, but instead as the beginning of an ongoing, lifelong process.

Let's view it as though we are, indeed, planting a "love garden" with the expectation that we will freely share its produce, its fruit, its beauty with others. Each time you share the bounty, you could touch a person deeply even if you never see him again, or you could develop a genuine friendship that will last a lifetime. In either case, and regardless of the duration, there has to be a starting point. And whether your new life of loving turns into meaningful relationships or days filled with dozens of unexpected smiles, isn't that better than living every day in a state of isolation? Wouldn't you rather live in a beautiful garden than a featureless desert? I sincerely hope your life is full and you are happy. If it is, then you've tasted the fruit of positively engaging with other people. Our world needs more people like you.

My entire goal and hope in writing this book is for our world to blend together in harmony with itself. I am convinced this can and will happen when we are willing to open ourselves up to each other with the solitary agenda of sharing our loving nature with anyone and everyone. That is the how of this equation. This chapter will go into more detail about the ways we can reach outside of ourselves in love. Like everything else in life, there are right ways and wrong ways to make things happen. What might work in one instance may not work in the next. I believe if genuine love is our motivation, our methods will fit the situation. Love has a way of refining sincerity. When someone recognizes love in you, they will be far more prepared to hear what you have to say. We know what we want to do. Now, let's figure out how we're going to do it.

The previous chapter described some of the different types of people and situations that we will typically encounter in our lives. I have no doubt you could think of even more variations that could be more appropriate to your own situation. My goal was to touch on the typical scenarios we either live with, work with, or might encounter frequently. Obviously, everyone's life puts them in their own unique environments.

As we begin to discuss how we are going to put loving encounters into our world, some of us will be ahead of the curve and are already doing what I've been talking about. Others may agree, in principle, that what I'm suggesting could make a significant difference, but would rather start by observing and learning to recognize the many manifestations of our love-starved culture I've been talking about. If we were at a "Don't Miss Love" seminar (there aren't any, by the way), and part of the seminar included breaking up into focus groups in which we would role-play some of the more common scenarios, that might be okay. But we're not so you're just going to have to start small and see how it goes on your own.

Before we get started with the how, there are a few important things to keep in mind. First, don't ever believe you have a finite amount of love to give away and be concerned that just when you start to get the hang of it, you'll suddenly have an empty "love tank." Earlier in the book, I described love as an inexhaustible resource, like an aquifer. In case you are not familiar with the word, aquifer is a variation of the word that describes groundwater. Both refer to the accumulation of water lying underground. The basic distinction between the two is that groundwater is water still in the process of slowly trickling downward through the soil. Eventually, it reaches natural formations capable of storing extremely large amounts of water, at which point it is referred to as an aquifer. How much water are we talking about? A lot! The U.S. Geological Survey (USGS) estimates the total amount of fresh water in the world's groundwater/aquifers to be 2,526,000 cubic miles. That's not an easy number to wrap your brain around. By the way, as astonishing as this is, it's only 0.8% of the earth's total water and only about 30% of the total amount of fresh water, the rest being above ground in lakes, rivers and streams, etc. I don't think they're counting swimming pools. Love is like an aquifer, not your checking account. Love doesn't have a quantity. It just is, like air or sunlight. You will never give all love away.

It's also very important to be prepared for how, or even if, your love will be received. You have to be prepared for the possibility that it won't be received at all, at least not by everybody. The first time you decide to reach outside yourself in love, they may react as if you don't even exist and completely ignore you. First of all, don't take it personally. When people don't return your attempt to show love, whether it's a greeting or trying to strike up a friendly conversation, they might not be paying attention, and sometimes they truly are ignoring you. Why is not your concern. All you can do is keep walking and be ready with a smile for the next person. A lot of people listen to music through ear buds that are hard to spot. When someone doesn't react, they may not have heard you. Other times people clearly hear you or notice your smile but stare at you as if you've suddenly grown a second head. Others will return your greeting with a mumble or grunt. But most people will smile and return your greeting, and the loving exchange has been made. In that couple of seconds, our world is a tiny bit friendlier than it would have been otherwise.

While I will typically greet people with at least a smile and, if I am able to make eye contact, a greeting, my motive when the timing is right, is to engage people in a brief conversation. Understand that I don't walk down the street trying to strike up a conversation with every person I meet. That would be kind of weird (even to me), and besides, who has that kind of time? When I'm traveling from, let's say, where I work to where I'll have lunch, I try to be aware of the people I meet on the sidewalk. When our paths cross, I smile and say good afternoon. Simple right? At the restaurant, I try to be more engaging. I ask the server how their day is going or what their plans are for the weekend. I'm not being nosy, I'm showing interest.

Ninety-nine times out of a hundred, my questions are well received, and I've created another loving exchange. The next time I visit the same place, the exchange is renewed and the friendly bond is made a little stronger.

As you start to lovingly interact with other people, you'll get all kinds of reactions and responses. Just know going in that love isn't always well received. There are some troubled, unhappy people in our world. If you smile and say good morning to one of them, the ice may be too thick to break through. That's okay. If enough people act in love towards these people, I believe they will begin to thaw. Again, why they react the way they do is not our concern. We are only there to give our love away. How they receive it is up to them alone.

Remember, boundaries must be respected. As I mentioned, you will try to love people who simply aren't interested. When, not if, this happens, you can never be confrontational. Does the following statement sound loving? "Hey! I just said good morning to you. What, are you too good for me?" Obviously not, especially if they pull out an ear bud because they didn't hear what you said in the first place. When you're ignored, move on to the next person.

There are also personal boundaries. When you're engaging with a man or woman, these boundaries are dynamic. As a man, I have to make instant and correct judgments about what those boundaries are when I am interacting with a woman. For example, having a friendly conversation with a female server at lunch is much different than initiating a conversation with a woman I happen to meet while walking back from lunch. Quite justifiably, women have their guard up when they're in public. What I intend as a friendly greeting could be perceived quite differently by a woman on the sidewalk. The solution is to have your eyes and heart wide open and your brain in the "on" position. In time, you'll become much better at reading each situation and knowing when to keep it very simple. It's important to remember that when you're truly acting in genuine love, a natural sincerity should be evident to the recipient. Regardless, even love must be tempered with common sense.

As we go forward with our goal of creating a friendlier, more loving world, remember that each and every time we have a genuine loving encounter with someone, we are contributing to that goal. You have not failed if you go an entire month without even a single friendly response to your loving ovations. Love is cumulative. As it begins to permeate our many different cultures and societies, our world will slowly become a better place. It has taken a long time for this world to become what it is today. Therefore it only makes sense it's not going to change over night. But if you're in a poorly lit room, turning out more lights isn't going to make the room any brighter. We have all been blessed with an abundance of our supreme emotion, love. And no matter how much it may have been repressed in us, it's still in there. Every time we draw from this incredible, inexhaustible resource, we are making the room a little brighter. So there is a strategy for how to love others better. I hope we all feel like we're part of something much bigger and far more important than any one of us. We can do it. You can do it. Let love be your guide.

If you're new to the loving concept of this book, there are some ways to get started without putting yourself out on a limb. My first suggestion is to start with someone you know and perhaps already love. As I pointed out before, our immediate family should be our most accessible recipients. After all, we see them every day, sometimes all day. I wouldn't necessarily tell them what you're doing because, it could create the uncomfortable dynamic of them expecting you to act in a certain way that you may not be ready for yet. Hopefully, they will begin to notice positive changes in your behavior. If you have already discussed the content of this book, it's something you could undertake together. You can compare notes around the dinner table. If you live alone, practice on your friends or the people you work with.

So what are you supposed to be practicing? Our first exercise is pretty simple. Are you ready? Smile at people. I know...what a concept! But it's a great place to start. When we genuinely smile, it lets people know what's happening inside. You don't even have to say anything. You get up in the morning and smile at your wife and children and say good morning. Hopefully, this won't be the first time you've ever done this. If you're not the smiling type, you can change that. You may have to start by smiling at yourself in the mirror, which might feel a bit strange at first. Or think of the times someone has taken your picture. What do they say just before they take the picture? "Everybody frown!" Of course not, they tell you to smile and you do it. The next time you see another member of your family, pretend like they're about to take your picture and smile.

Once you've mastered smiling at your loved ones, you're ready to smile at people you don't love, or may not even know. I call it the "pre-emptive smile." At first, that's all you have to do; you walk on to the bus and smile at the driver and, if you're so inclined, say good morning. You smile at the person sitting next to you. Again, some of these people may not return your smile, and that's okay. Suppose you drive to work instead of taking public transportation. If another driver happens to look in your direction, give them a smile. Pedestrians are also good, since they usually try to make eye contact with drivers when they're about to cross the street. When they do, give them a smile. As you become more comfortable with smiling at others, I hope you start to notice a subtle change beginning to take place in yourself. You may start to feel a tiny bit more relaxed and perhaps your mood will improve slightly. What's even better about this is that as you have been smiling at others and your mood has improved, the same thing may be happening in the people you smiled at. You don't know what's going on in other peoples' lives. For some people, receiving a simple, genuine smile could make a difference in their day. Even a simple smile from a stranger could be the personal connection they really needed at that moment. For you it was a simple act, but for them it could mean everything. Never underestimate the significance of your smile.

Assuming you've realized it's okay to smile at other people, especially ones you don't know, let's talk about how you might go to the next level of encounter, words. Remember I referred to the first level, smiling, as the preemptive smile. While I believe that in itself should be considered a loving exchange (even if the other person doesn't smile back) it can also be preliminary to a slightly deeper encounter. Every situation is different. In some, taking the step from a smile to a conversation could be difficult or awkward. For example, striking up a friendly conversation with some one you meet walking on a sidewalk would be awkward at best and disconcerting, perhaps even alarming, for the other person. I will usually attempt a genial conversation with someone if we're both waiting to cross the street. Sometimes the other person is very open to talking. Others, not so much. Just like smiling, if they don't welcome your friendly engagement, it's alright. You can still wish them a good day. Our goal is to increase the number of positive, friendly encounters in our day. You have still accomplished that even if it only goes in one direction.

So how would this conversation start? I'll give you some examples that essentially cover the typical responses you may receive.

Talking to a statue:
"Good morning! How's your day going?"
No response.
"What a beautiful day we're having."

Blank stare.

"Well, have a good day."

They're already halfway across the street ahead of you.

Monosyllabic conversation

"Good morning! How's your day going?"

"Okay" (Sorry, that's two syllables)

"What a beautiful day we're having."

"Yeah"

"Well, have a good day."

"Yeah"

Red flag conversation

"Good morning! How's your day going?"

"Who me? Pretty darn good. How do you do?"

"Well it's a good day, thank you."

"That's so awesome! Hey would you like to come over for dinner?"

"Uhm well...it's kind of you to offer, thanks. But I'll say no this time."

"Really? I'm a good cook. Hey, do you like Sponge Bob?"

"Friend, I hope you have an excellent day."

"He lives in a pineapple under the sea. Did you know that?"

"Yes, I do know that. So long."

Actual conversation

"Good morning! How's your day going?"

"Pretty good so far. How's yours?"

"Not bad, thank you."

"Good"

"Don't you love the weather we're having?"

"It's awesome. Who says it always rains in Portland?"

"Everybody who doesn't live here, but that's okay. It's getting too crowded."

"You can say that again."

"Well, have a good rest of your day."

"And you as well."

Even though you would have felt differently about each conversation (especially the third one), each would have been a valid attempt and would have qualified as another instance of you giving love to another person. I include the "Red Flag" conversation so you'll be aware that sometimes the person you say hello to may not be playing with a full deck. Sometimes it's hard to tell. But the point I want to make is that I wouldn't let this chance encounter, albeit somewhat disconcerting (and maybe kind of amusing), make you shy away from the much more likely possibility you will have a normal encounter. Clearly, the last example would have been the most fulfilling. And really, the duration of that conversation was about right. Again, keeping in mind that we have to be sensitive to the other peoples' boundaries, to try and lengthen that particular conversation could have been a bit too much. It all depends on the situation. If you're waiting for the light to change so you can enter the crosswalk, the length and content were about right. If you're sitting next to this person on the bus, longer could be acceptable. But only as long as the other person seems to welcome it. You have to be sensitive to the body language of the other person and respond accordingly. The main thing is that regardless of the duration, be friendly and sincere. Remember, we're trying to melt ice with a candle, not a flame thrower.

Another common situation that presents itself is your work environment. Obviously, the type of work you do can affect this dramatically. You're not as likely to have a friendly, engaging conversation out on the floor of a steel mill like you would in an office setting. But in either case, the opportunity will arise. When it does, take advantage of it. The majority of jobs will include people working in close proximity to each other. In these typical scenarios, we will have many opportunities to cultivate healthy relationships. I do understand there can be an abundance of issues in work situations. For every personality, there is a different dynamic. Some personality types will naturally blend together, while others are going to clash. It's no different out in the rest of our world. With that in mind, I have some suggestions for how you can approach the people you work with in love.

First of all, if you pray, say a prayer. I promise you, the God of love wants us to act in love towards each other. Ask him to show you ways to share genuine love with your coworkers. You may be surprised at how this prayer will be answered. If you're not a praying person, think about the type of workplace you would like to work in and shape your approach around what you would like to see happen. If your vision is one where everybody gets along, it'll be a mistake to be inconsistent in how you treat people. Everybody must be a recipient of your pre-emptive smile and any positive direction it takes thereafter.

Whether you pray about it or not, friendly sincerity must be at the heart of your demeanor. You can't act like you're trying to win the office popularity contest, nor should you come off as the office schmoozer. Some could say there's a fine line between acting like you "love" everybody and being a phony. On the surface, that could appear to be the case. But as I began to think more about the concept of not missing love, I also began to realize it may take a fundamental change in how we treat each other. A naturally sincere, open and engaging person may be a rare commodity in our society, but whether these people are a dying breed or not, it doesn't mean people who aren't like them can't naturally develop the essence of what these people bring to the table. If your motive each day is to share genuine love with anybody and everybody, if that is the foundation upon which you build your day, your mood won't be the same as someone who doesn't care one way or another if he shows love or not. How you treat other people will be pure. Will this be a different you than what your coworkers are used to? Maybe, maybe not. But whether it is or not, the results of your sincerity will be welcomed.

After a few weeks or months of practicing these two simple principles of preemptively smiling and initiating the occasional casual conversation, you will no doubt have become better at it. I am hopeful you will have noticed your own world is a little better, maybe a little softer around the edges. As this has been happening, you may also have become a sort of "love advocate." Maybe someone has noticed a change in you. If so, you might get the chance to explain what has been contributing to the positive changes in your mood and what lies at the heart of those changes. This is an important time. When this conversation takes place, and it may be one you initiate, the person you are talking to is at a crossroads. Especially if they can clearly see the impact it has had on you, they may be interested in trying it themselves. If and when that happens, our world has just gotten one person closer to becoming a better place.

In the previous chapter, we discussed a variety of people who deserve our loving engagement. As we get further into the "how" of our loving concept, I hope you realize that whether you're interacting with a guy on the street, a coworker, or another driver, the basics are pretty much the same. You will certainly understand early on, regardless of how your encounters come about, they will all start with some fairly basic behavior.

You will smile and perhaps have a brief conversation. How you got there shouldn't be all that different whether the person is covered in tattoos or the president of a bank (In Portland, sometimes that can be the same person). The point is that even though there are some decidedly different types of people, none should be missed, and how you initiate your encounter shouldn't change much. You don't need to have a different smile for a homeless person and yet another for one of your work mates. If it's genuine, a smile is a smile. However, the difference in these encounters is the situation and context. I want to stress the importance of using common sense and good judgment when you decide to engage someone beyond your smile. If you're a man and you're walking home one night and happen to encounter a woman just getting out of her car, smile and say good evening. That's all. Do I have to tell you how counterproductive it would be to try and engage this woman in a conversation? Every single scenario is different. And while you should see everyone with your heart of love, you must use your brain just as much. Don't undermine your loving intentions with inappropriate words or bad timing. If you are a woman, smiling at someone, even a man, doesn't necessarily tell them you're any easy target. On the contrary, it says you are a woman with self-confidence, that you're not afraid to look someone in the eyes.

There are still a couple of things worth discussing as we explore how we approach life with a loving perspective. You have no doubt heard the term "non-verbal communication." For me, this has more than one meaning. Typically, the term is used to describe our body language and what can generally be read into our facial expressions or our body positions. Having your arms crossed is a common one. This tells people you are uncomfortable or have your guard up (or you're chilly). Whenever I see this, I immediately believe, for what ever reason, the other person isn't one-hundred percent on board with me or what I'm talking about. I once had a job interview in which the interviewer sat with her arms crossed during the entire interview. Needless to say, this did not fill me with much confidence. When we were finished (by then, I had already decided the job wasn't for me anyway), I pointed out to the woman what she had been doing and the message it sent my way. She was unaware she'd even been doing it. This is one reason why it's so important to have a ready smile. A smile can diffuse a situation pretty fast, or at least open the door for an amiable connection. In her case, my friendly demeanor during the interview didn't seem to change anything. But it would have been a mistake for me to match her stance with an equally restrained form of non-verbal communication. It's usually better to have an engaging smile than reflect someone else's discomfort. There are many manifestations of non-verbal communication. It would take a trained psychiatrist to identify and interpret them all. Therefore, your consistent, open, amiable countenance is always going to be an important part of the equation. Don't confuse the issue by adding your own misunderstood body language. Yours should say love.

Let's say you want to get on board the "love train" and today's the day. However, you're not completely convinced you have the personality skills that will work. Your day starts like every other, but what you're about to attempt almost feels weird. Inevitably you will come to the place where your "love train" is about to make its first stop. With your less than convinced mindset, you might approach your first candidate with a demeanor that says you're not quite ready for this. If you're nervously making intermittent eye contact between your "target audience" and the sidewalk, your eventual smile might make it look more like you just wet your pants, than "How's your day going?" Before you've had a chance to have whatever kind of interaction you were planning, your candidate has side-stepped you like a land mine on a tuna sandwich.

The truth is some of us aren't as prepared as others to reach out in love. For this reason, I suggest you practice beforehand on your family and friends. By doing this first, you'll be able to step into the other parts of your world more relaxed and better prepared for constructive interactions. After you have practiced for a while and are better prepared, you will be far more likely to project a sense of friendly confidence. Eventually, even your non-verbal communication will say you are friendly and approachable. More importantly, that will be a reflection of what is actually going on inside you. My hope is after having multiple loving exchanges with other people, you will have an inner peace that is plain to see on the outside.

One more important thing. There are plenty of people in our world with personalities that make them uncomfortable engaging with strangers. That's okay. If you fit that description, there are still ways you can participate. Here's an alternative. Since you may, indeed, be more reserved, you may also be one of the people I meet occasionally who seem to be ignoring me when I say hello or smile. In your case, you're not being rude or disinterested, you're just being your normal reserved self. So what you can do instead of looking away? Respond with a smile or a hello. You didn't initiate the contact, but if you really want to start learning how to open up to people, or at least be part of a more positive and open world, a friendly reply is a good way to start. And even if you maintain your reserved nature for the rest of your life, you can still be part of the solution.

One other kind of communication that I would only classify as non-verbal is the way we communicate while we're driving our cars. I am, of course, not referring to talking on our cell phones and especially not about texting while we drive (don't get me started on that one). What I'm referring to are the subtle, and sometimes not so subtle, ways we exchange our "thoughts and desires" to other drivers. As I pointed out earlier, there's something peculiar about how many of us become different people when we get behind the wheel. Some of us become adversarial. We drive as if we

104

can suddenly read the minds of every other driver and we know what they're really trying to get away with.

Here's a typical scenario of "vehicular mind reading." You're driving along, minding your own business, when another driver moves into your lane (because, well you really do own that lane as long as you're driving in it) without using his turn signal! You say to yourself, "Oh, so that's how you're going to play it. I see. Sure, let's just barge our way into that guy's lane. He'll make room for me. I'm special." The whole time you're having this ridiculous conversation with yourself, the other guy is actually saying to himself, "Did I turn off the coffee maker? I think I did. Maybe I should call my wife and ask her. No wait, don't they have automatic shut-off? Yeah, that's it. No problem...Say, why is that guy behind me waving his arms around?"

If this other person had used his turn signal, would you have slowed down a bit to let him move into "your lane"? If you're the person I've been urging you to become for the past seven chapters, you would have. And you would have done it with a smile and a wave.

Now let's contrast the same basic scenario as it might transpire in a more "pedestrian" setting. You're at work and remember you need to go see somebody about something. You leave your office and start down the hall. You're walking, minding your own business, when somebody comes out of his office and doesn't look to see if anyone is coming. You manage to avoid each other and the other guy says, "Oh, I'm sorry. I should look before I leap." Would your reasonable response be to shove the guy against the wall and say, "Watch where you're going next time! Who taught you how to walk anyway?" Or maybe not. Unless you're insane, you'd probably say something like, "No worries, Bill. I was in kind of a hurry. How are you doing today? Did you get that Fleebermayer contract?"

So why should essentially the same situations have such dramatically different responses just because one took place while we were driving? I believe it's because, in the driving example, any hope of being able to respond to the same basic "inconvenience" has been undermined by the contrary, adversarial mindset we allow ourselves to have when we get behind the wheel.

Is there a possibility we can actually transform ourselves, our society, into one where the members live respectfully and lovingly towards each other? Is it possible every part of our lives, including the part we spend driving our cars, could be friendlier and more peaceful? Could driving even become safer and less stressful? You know I believe it can. As for my own inability to always overlook the things people do behind the wheel, before I even start my car, I think about what I'm about to do and how I am going to do it peacefully and safely. I am going to assume other drivers aren't out to best me at every turn, and what they're actually doing is going to work or the store without any agenda other than getting to work or the store. If somebody waves for you to pull in front of them, give them a courtesy wave. People in Japan have started substituting two flashes of their tail lights for the courtesy wave. It's a good idea and I have adopted it as well.

There are plenty of ways we can make friendly, non-aggressive connections with people in other cars. Most of it depends on your mindset. Whether you agree with me or not about how many of us go through a transformation behind the wheel, you must see some odd behavior during your commute from time to time. Are you seeing a corresponding type of behavior in people when you're not driving? Not really? That's my point. Something happens in our brains. I see a similar thing happen at Costco. There are some people who, as soon as they show their Costco card at the front door, drift into a sort of subliminal condition I call the "Costco Fog." In their minds, it's like everybody else in the store has suddenly disappeared and they're walking around in this giant warehouse by themselves and their shopping posse. Put these same people in any other store and they're in and out, getting on with their day. However, put them inside a Costco, it's a Thorazine waltz, shopping cart firmly ensconced in the middle of the aisle, not missing a single sample lady. I want so badly to bring an air horn from my boat with me some day. It would, of course, be called a "Costco Fog Horn." Someday I'm going to follow one of these people outside and see how they drive their car. There must be a connection.

For every single person and situation, there will be a best-case scenario on how we can make a loving connection. It would be impossible to try and describe every possibility in this book. But regardless of the details, every one of these "hows" must begin within us before we even walk out the front door. Just watch the evening news. Could our world use more love and less strife? Yes, of course. Is a world of less strife going to suddenly start happening on its own? It sure doesn't look that way. One of the definitions of an insane person is when someone believes if they keep doing the same thing over and over, they can expect to get different results. While I don't believe we are exhibiting characteristics of insanity, there does seem to be a tacit belief that our world, our human condition is just going to fix itself. I, for one, don't want to wait to find out.

Starting with your personal decision that you are willing and capable of making a contribution to positive change, your world might just begin to be transformed from apathy to empathy. You must make this decision for yourself to be part of improving our lot. Once you've done it, don't keep it to yourself. There's nothing complicated about getting started. Just start going through your day with a ready smile for others. If you get a chance to interact with them beyond a smile, go for it. I am absolutely convinced every time this takes place, your world will become just a little bit nicer. As you build on that and it begins to happen more and more, your days will become a bit softer and, at the end of the day, you might just feel more relaxed. The more of us taking part in this, the better. Every time even one of us is willing to lower the barriers separating us from each other, this world becomes less adversarial and more functional.

How you choose to love others is up to you. I have suggested some simple ways that have worked for me. Just keep it simple, but be consistent in your effort. I promise you, some people will not give a hoot about whether you love them or not. But those people are in the minority. If they want to live in an apathetic world, fine. But I don't, and I don't believe you do either. In the next chapter, we will go over some things we should avoid in showing love for others. For now, I hope you feel more equipped to move forward into what I hope will be life with more smiles, softer edges and maybe a few new friends along the way. How you decide to share the very real overabundance of love you possess is a personal decision. It's a personal decision to even share at all. But every time you make the choice to give some of it away, you have thrown another log on the fire that will overwhelm the chill of isolation and apathy in our world. This is the kind of "global warming" I don't think anyone will argue about.

This chapter has given you some practical advice on how you can get started, or become more comfortable with sharing your loving nature. As with anything, there can be some pitfalls if you're not paying attention. The next chapter will give you some tools to use as you're getting started with your noble endeavor.

1. Give your definition of a "Love Garden."

2. Do you agree with the author when he says love is an inexhaustible resource?

3. Why must boundaries play a big part in sharing love with others?

4. Why should we start with a smile?

5. Have each member of the group participate in role playing one of the four different conversation examples.

6. How could an open, loving environment change your workplace?

7. What are some examples of non-verbal communication, from either direction, that could short-circuit love?

8. Do you agree with the author's belief that some people change when they get behind the wheel?

9. Do you agree with the author's belief that our world will not improve on its own?

10. Why does it feel so good to give?

8
Making Mistakes Doesn't Mean Stop Trying

"Every strike brings me closer to the next home run."
Babe Ruth

We all have experience doing the right thing for the wrong reason. The following true story is a good example of this. This man, a pastor who would normally look at the circumstances from a different point of view, was blinded by haste and his own human nature.

Pastor Roger Nishioka had just returned late in the evening to his home in Atlanta after a short, but jam-packed speaking engagement. Due to the late hour, he decided to pick up something for dinner. He stopped at a small grocery store near his home and quickly found what he needed. He approached the only open check-out stand to find the clerk helping an elderly patron who apparently didn't have quite enough to cover her purchases. The clerk was checking prices and taking items off until she was able to cover it. The process was taking a lot of time. Anxious to get home, Pastor Nishioka was getting impatient and decided to see if he could speed things along.

With unmistakable exasperation, he looked at the clerk and asked, "So how much is she short?"

"I'm not sure yet." The clerk answered with some frustration. The pastor pulled twenty dollars from his wallet and quickly handed it to the clerk. "Just cover the rest with this."

"Um...Okay." The clerk glanced between the woman and the pastor and finished bagging the rest of the woman's groceries. "Do you want the change?" the clerk asked holding out his hand towards the pastor.

Feeling pretty self-righteous about his magnanimous gesture, the pastor replied, "Just give the rest to her." The woman accepted the money, carefully put it in her pocketbook and, without a word, started to slowly walk away from the checkout stand.

The clerk turned towards the woman and said, "Hey, this guy just paid for your food. Can't you at least say thanks?"

The woman turned and, after a glance at the clerk, looked directly at the pastor for a moment before saying, "You never even looked at me." After a few moments, she turned and walked towards the exit.

The clerk, mouth open watched the woman walk away. "Hey, that's pretty rude-"

Suddenly feeling the pain of regret, the pastor reached out and gently touched the arm of the clerk. "No son, she's right. I did that for me, not for her." The pastor paid for his things and, with a waning smile at the clerk, started towards the parking lot and home.

The right thing for the wrong reason. His impatient determination to get home undermined his pastor's heart. Under different circumstances, he most likely would have seen the desperate situation the woman was in and looked her in the eyes with love, insisting on paying her debt. No doubt, the pastor learned a valuable lesson that day. You could say his loving nature had been short circuited.

So why would a pastor fail to act in love from the very beginning of this situation? I think part of the reason was the context. The encounter at the grocery store happened when the man was trying to get home after a long trip out of town. Within that context, he didn't think of it any differently than the inconvenience of having to stop at a series of red lights or having to wait for his luggage. His focus was on his hunger and on getting home, not on who he might be able to bless. And you could ask why, with a pastor's heart for other people, shouldn't his focus have been on the woman rather than on meeting his own needs? And the answer-he is a human. And humans, whether they're pastors or regular folks, will all fall prey to human nature. I can assure you there have been plenty of times when this pastor has done the right thing.

Reading a story about a pastor getting his "love wires crossed" could be a bit disconcerting. After all, if he's a pastor, essentially a "professional love conduit," what hope do we have as regular people? Well, I guarantee, like that pastor, you won't be perfect. As we begin our pursuit of a more loving world, it's highly likely we'll do something kind of awkward. This is especially true if this whole sharing love thing is new to you. But with practice, you'll become more comfortable with your approach. You may find out pretty quickly that even when you are in the best mood ever, it's definitely not a good idea to just walk up to a complete stranger and give them a hug and tell them they're awesome. In fact, I would like to tell you right now to not ever do that! If they're a loved one or a close friend, go for it. Otherwise, keep your head on straight and your hands to yourself.

What are some of the other things that could happen you will wish hadn't? This is actually a difficult question, because there are as many possibilities as there are personalities. What works for one person, may not work for another. In spite of this, there are a few things to look out for. One I already mentioned; being confrontational with someone who seems to have snubbed your attempt to share love. As you begin to devote more brain cells, and more of your heart, to loving other people, you'll begin to notice things about people you hadn't noticed before. Instead of not really noticing what people are doing while they walk down the street or through the office at work, you might start to see them differently. You'll notice some people never look at you, or, for that matter, even seem to be looking at anything. In World War II, they called it the "thousand-yard stare." This term referred to soldiers suffering from extreme cases of battle fatigue. Today, people who seem to be completely tuned out to their surroundings most likely are not suffering from battle fatigue. Some do it as a defense mechanism; they may assume if they avoid eye contact, they can avoid having to interact with other people. Others are truly "out to lunch" and are not even trying to be aware of what is happening around them.

The mistake, and it would be a big one, is to confront these people when they appear to be ignoring you. In some cases, they really are ignoring you. In others, they're just not paying attention or they're preoccupied. In either case, you absolutely cannot confront them about the perceived snub. People can be very emotionally fragile. Being confrontational for any reason is not good. To raise a fuss because they didn't smile back at you would even be worse. Just know going in that your job, if you want to call it that, is to extend yourself in a friendly and loving way to everyone. But at the same time, know that even if you pass your love on to another person, it's still love even if it bounces off of the intended recipient. You've done your part by initiating the contact. If it is well received and given back, so much the better. But even if the entire process starts and ends with your smile, you have still succeeded. Sometimes you just have to leave it at that.

I hope what I am saying doesn't raise red flags for anyone who's considering the adoption of a more loving nature. Every situation is different. Every place we choose to be loving is different. For example, it would not be a good idea for anybody to walk down a dark alley in the hopes of being able to share your friendly nature. In most cities, there really isn't any good reason to go down a dark alley. My advice is to be your loving self where you feel most comfortable and secure. That can be in your own home, your neighborhood, or your place of work or leisure. The more comfortable you are with your surroundings, the easier it will be for you to share your loving nature.

Earlier in the book I talked about respecting others' boundaries. For some people, these boundaries are quite big. Some boundaries are physical while others are emotional. In regards to physical boundaries, the map is all over the place. If you're a Seinfeld fan, you may remember the "Close Talker" episode when actor Judge Reinhold had the annoying habit of wanting to be about six inches away when he talked with you. That's a bit close for anybody. But you don't have to be a close talker to make someone feel like you're invading their space. When you're interacting with a stranger, and especially a member of the opposite sex, you must give people breathing room. It would be a mistake to cross these lines when all you're trying to do is smile and say hello. And again, men, I have to stress the importance of really respecting those boundaries when you interact with women. Equally, women must be cautious with men.

I spend a fair amount of time observing how strangers interact with one another. One of the things I've noticed is that women are less likely to make eye contact with men they don't already know. I'm sure many avoid eye contact with some men they do know. They all have their own reasons for doing this, but it should be obvious to anyone, and especially men, that in today's culture woman have good reason to keep their guard up. In our sexually charged world, women have every right to presume the worst about any man they encounter on the street. I believe most of the time, a man who smiles at a woman doesn't have an ulterior motive. He's just being a friendly human, and there's nothing wrong with that. But the woman has no way to know this. So if you are a guy and you greet a woman walking towards you with a smile and she completely ignores you, don't take it personally. On the other hand, if she does respond in a similarly friendly way, it does not mean she's interested and the door is now open for your pursuit. You smiled, she smiled back. Great, now walk on and enjoy the pleasant micro moment you just had. Remember, gentlemen, while she has every right to respond however she chooses, you also have every right to be friendly to her or anybody else. That doesn't give you the right to be a knucklehead.

Emotional boundaries, on the other hand, aren't quite as obvious. Clearly, non-verbal communication can reveal how a person is responding emotionally. But sometimes people are pretty good at masking their discomfort. An example of non-verbal communication within this context would be a complete lack of response from someone you pass on the street. They are giving you signals, without speaking, that they have no intention of responding to you in any way. As you reach outside yourself, you'll become better at reading people by their posture towards you or the look on their faces. When you see this, respect their wishes and keep moving.

Sometimes you could be having what seems like a positive interaction with someone and not realize that, for them, it is not very positive. It would have to be more than a passing interaction for this to materialize. But even after a few minutes, you should be able to read between the lines and grasp that this person who seems to be open to your friendly overtures, is actually not so comfortable. This is another reason to keep things short with strangers. If deeper interaction is going to happen, it may take more than one time. If it's meant to be, the occasion will arise again. If not, don't force your friendly nature on someone who doesn't really welcome it, regardless of how they appear to be receiving it.

There is another possible misstep in our desire to share our loving nature with others that really needs to be mentioned. This is something that was actually brought to my attention by a loved one and, in fact, I was the one making the mistake. I am so very thankful this was pointed out to me. Here's what I was doing. In my earnest desire to be a loving, engaging person, I was not paying attention to someone very dear to me, who I happened to be with at the time. My focus had been on others, and I ignored my dear friend.

I think I've made it pretty clear how I feel about how our "devices" can come between us. In this case, I was essentially doing the same thing by allowing my good intentions to come between myself and someone who is a very dear friend. There really isn't much difference, is there? If I had realized at the time what I was doing, I would have "hung up" and returned my focus to the person I was with. I'll get plenty of opportunities to extend my loving nature to other people. But when I do, I must pay attention to the dynamics of the moment. If I'm with a friend, I am obliged to stay by their side, as a friend. When I talk with someone else, especially if I sense love is missing from this person's life, I should never forego my responsibility as a true friend for the sake of another. Anyone who knows me knows going in that I have a propensity to open myself to virtually anyone. However, I am making a mistake if it preempts the solidarity and significance of a strong friendship.

How can we avoid this? First, pay attention. Don't forget who you are, where you are and who you're with. If you see an opportunity to be a caring person, be a caring person. Just don't do it alone. If you feel so inclined, have some cards printed with your contact information on them. If it feels right, hand out a card. Especially if this new person notices your devotion to the person you're already with, it tells them something important about you-you can be trusted.

Perhaps one of the biggest mistakes we're all making is to assume, given the borderline reclusive disposition of stranger-to-stranger contact these days, that we should all keep our smiles to ourselves. How is this approach working out for us so far? In my opinion, not very well. Ever expanding numbers of people, young and old, walk along staring at their cell phones, tuned out to their surroundings and to the very real life happening around them. Friends sit across the table from each other in restaurants deep in conversation, but with someone else on the other end of their phones. Go for a commute on a light rail train and there is virtually no conversation except when friends happen to be riding together.

We live on a big planet with billions of other people. We are already separated by continents, countries, cities and neighborhoods. We are divided by age, race, religion and economics. We are separated by social norms, appearances, and misperceptions. In spite of all of this disparity, we all still live on the same blue marble traveling through space and time. It's a mistake to intentionally close ourselves off, no matter how subtly, from other people. If we could be in Omaha standing two feet away from another person and be no more likely to have a friendly interaction with them than if they were in Calcutta, we're all missing out. I believe it is a mistake for a child to be raised with the belief they should essentially ignore everybody else in their world. While no parent would literally say that to their child, many will demonstrate it on a daily basis. What do our children learn when they watch us react in anger to the slightest, unintended offense rather than responding with a smile? Think about how confusing it must be for a child to try and figure out why dad waves and smiles at some people while he's driving, but other times he gets really mad and does that weird thing with his middle finger next to the window.

As I have been pointing out, even when our only aim is to be friendly and open to other people, mistakes in how it transpires can take place. I would call them innocent missteps from a well-intended heart. If this happens to someone enough, it could be discouraging perhaps to the point they might stop trying all together. I don't think that will happen though. Here's why: love is the one pure emotion capable of overcoming even the most inadequate attempts to share it ("Love covers a multitude of sins." 1 Peter 4:8, NIV). You're giving away something of value most will gladly accept and, hopefully, pass on. Consider the alternative. If you're angry, not necessarily at any particular person or thing, and you're around other people, do they sense your anger, embrace it, and then at some point pass it on to someone else? Sometimes. While anger and hatred repel other people, sometimes, the mood transfers to others. Then there are two angry people.

A genuine, unencumbered expression of love well given, on the other hand, will rarely be rebuffed. If you smile at a stranger, they're not likely to run in the opposite direction. Anger can't make the same statement, only love. The point I am making is that you need to know and accept that what you are trying to do has a compelling natural purity. If I am correct in my hypothesis that, as humans, we are naturally disposed to treat each other in love, what you are attempting should be as welcome as a breath of fresh air. Just be thoughtful and sensitive to who and where you are giving it. Love will take care of the rest.

The biggest mistake we can make in sharing our love is to not share our love. When this happens (as manifested in the current condition of our culture and world), nothing changes. When we don't share love, it is wasted. When we keep love bottled up inside, our exchanges, our interactions, lose their meaning beyond simple communication. Love is our bond. When we lose that connection, we are at the mercy of our human nature. When that happens, our world, our lives become vulnerable.

Think back to how the events of 9/11 affected our country. We were suddenly united like we hadn't been since the beginning of World War II. Our churches were full, people treated each other better. The very opposite of love made us emotionally and, for some, spiritually, circle the wagons and embrace each other against a common enemy of evil. In time, as all things do, our unity subsided and our divisions returned. The evil is still there. America is no less the "great Satan" in some people's eyes now than it was then. If anything, that same evil is even more organized now. The difference between then and now is that our common belief, our love of our country and our sorrow over too many lives lost has been replaced by apathy, preoccupation with technology and a self-centric culture.

The love standing in defiance to evil in 2001 is still within all of us. Will it take another world-shattering tragedy, or perhaps a steady flow of acts of terrorism to revive it in ourselves enough to see it in each other? We are mistaken if we willingly allow things to keep going as they are. It doesn't take tragedy to unite us in love. It takes a decision. It is one I have already made. I hope and pray you will join me.

If part of your decision has included following God as your Savior and guide through life, the next chapter will reveal some important things to consider as you walk your pathway to eternity. If you have not made that connection, read on. You may have some questions answered about church-goers. In either case, mistakes have been made.

1. How could Pastor Nishioka have acted differently to show his loving heart?

2. Should a pastor or other member of clergy be expected to act differently towards strangers?

3. How can being confrontational ruin your chance of showing love?

4. What are some ways we can be with a friend and still show love to others?

5. Why is it a mistake to keep love to ourselves?

6. Do you agree with the author's belief that our world needs each of us to open ourselves to others?

7. How do people share anger?

8. Relate a story of how people drew together on 9/11.

9. Why did the bonding effects of 9/11 fade so quickly?

9
Believing In Love

"Spread the good news, if all else fails, use words."
St. Francis of Assisi

Mary Lou Fore was a wonderful person. In fact, that's the predominant trait people remember about her. There were plenty of details to go along with her being wonderful, but add them all together and you still end up at...wonderful. I never heard her make a disparaging comment about another person. I don't know if she wasn't able to recognize it in others, or if she just chose to ignore the negative and focus on the good she saw instead.

Mary was a faithful and loving wife, mother, grandmother and friend. Certainly, much of her character could be attributed to good genes and an honest upbringing. More than that, she was who she was because of her strong faith in God. Once she accepted Christ as her Savior, she never looked back, never wavered. She allowed her faith to shape and mold her into an even better person. She truly was becoming the person God designed her to be from the beginning.

Perhaps one of the things that makes her stand out so profoundly in the hearts and memory of so many is that she accomplished this in just fifty-four years of life. She was taken from us by inflammatory breast cancer, a particularly deadly form of that disease. Even as she fought her losing battle, her faith never wavered. Only at the very end did her smile start to fade as the disease did its worst to her.

How did Mary manage to be wonderful for so many years to so many people? She knew who she was, and knew where she was going. She lived her faith without compromise. She didn't just act the part by putting on a Christian performance when she knew people were watching. She was Christlike. That's what being a Christian means.

Mary was also a loving sister of mine. She and my other sister, Sharon, and I, were raised by parents who did their best to model upright behavior. They introduced us to Jesus Christ and didn't walk away from teaching us and showing us what it meant to commit your life to something so precious and profound. But it was Mary who never seemed to wonder about what she might be missing outside of Christ. She recognized early on that Christ's was the right path and made a commitment to stay on it. I, on the other hand, and my older sister to a much lesser degree, had to find out for ourselves what lay down those other paths. Eventually we both realized Mary had been right all along. Her life was a pattern for believing in love, and she did it with joy and an open, accepting nature that was never compromised by her words or behavior.

Now as my own path has come full circle to my Christian foundations, it is clear to me when I weigh the significance of love in my own life, that there's an even more profound character to love when it is married to my commitment to the very Father of Love. But even without a personal commitment to God himself, I believe there is an undeniable connection between every member of humanity and his loving essence. I have also recognized there are people who do not agree with me. In fact, they don't agree with the existence of any higher power at all, loving or not. This chapter is for those of us who do embrace the belief that not only does

God exist, but that his loving nature is at the heart of our past, present and future. We believe Jesus Christ is his greatest expression of love and, ultimately, we will exist eternally in his loving presence. I will refer to these people simply as believers.

Because of these bedrock beliefs, believers are compelled to live a different kind of life during our time on earth. As we live out these beliefs, people are watching. And by what ever standard they happen to choose, the people watching will measure what they see and hear against what they think we should be doing. This can be problematic for both. First of all, the non-believer might be basing their evaluation on criteria that may or may not have any valid basis for comparison. In reality, unless the "observer" has had actual firsthand experience or genuine exposure to what truly lives in the heart of a believer, their opinion could be based on virtually anything from speculation, prejudice, and generalities, to just jumping on the skeptic band wagon. This would be no different than someone forming an opinion about golfers without ever setting foot on a golf course. If you are a non-believer, you may be jumping to completely unjustified conclusions about believers. This pre-programmed opinion could completely close the door that could one day open when you might want to test the waters of realistic spirituality for yourself.

This prejudiced approach by non-believers can also be less than fair to the believer. It is not a small thing to reach the conclusion that God is real and you have decided to live your life under the lordship of Christ. It's also not an easy life to live. In spite of the depth and dimensions of what led a believer to believe in the first place, as he strives to stay on that path, virtually anything he does can be misconstrued or misinterpreted in the eyes of the very people he wants most to influence, the non-believer. Admittedly, believers and non-believers are both guilty of pulling off some pretty questionable behavior. But it's when the believer does something kind of sketchy that the validity of everything they stand for is brought into question. Do you remember Jim and Tammy Faye Bakker? Jim Bakker, a televangelist, made some rather colossal mistakes that were put on display for the world to see. He, in fact, ended up in prison for a time. Naturally, his mistakes flavored the opinions of many people towards all Christians. See how those people are? They're all a bunch of hypocrites. But to compare what Jim Bakker did with the daily lives of millions of Christians wouldn't be that different from saying all Christian women must also wear entirely too much make-up. It's not fair, nor is it true. There are no doubt far worse examples of things done by believers that are regrettable. The same can be said of non-believers. Believers or not, we all live out our human nature.

As believers, we cannot ignore the disparity of us being judged as a group rather than as individuals. Is it fair? It doesn't matter. It's the way it is and it's up to us, with God's help, to exhibit genuine, Christ-like behavior as much as possible. If we can't, we're no better than anybody else. And that really is one of the keys we have to realize and accept in the first place, that we aren't better than anybody else. When it comes to our human nature, to our susceptibility to doing the wrong thing at the wrong time, we're all the same. The difference is in how we process what we do and what motivates us to be who we are. True believers have a different mindset as we process what life brings our way. We tend to think in relation to something bigger than ourselves instead of how things affect us personally. For us, God is the center of everything we hold dear. Without him, without his love, our lives would take on a completely different meaning.

If you are not a believer, I suppose you could skip reading the rest of this chapter. On the other hand, it may give you some insight into why we believers do what we do. You may be surprised by the number of similarities we share. You may relax some preconceived notions and even come to some different conclusions, or at least be open to the possibility.

In the last chapter, I referred to Pastor Nishioka as a "professional love conduit." This doesn't mean he has some kind of exclusive, secret ability to show his loving nature. In fact, I think he demonstrated that he is as fallible as the rest of us. But of all people, shouldn't we expect a pastor to be more tuned into the ins and outs of how love works? All pastors presumably devote more time to the business of charitable love than lay people. That's part of what we're paying them to do, right? Very few people go into ministry because of what they get paid. Their main motivation should be love, not money or notoriety. For many, something profound took place in their life that lit a fire for love and compassion. For some people, this passion can only be fulfilled by a devoted life of serving others. Some would say they have been "called into the ministry" by God himself.

So why don't all believers hear God call them into the ministry? Actually, I think we are all called into a ministry. It's just that some people are led to a career more specifically devoted to the actual ministry of serving in a church setting. Even within this context, and depending on the size of the church, there are differing responsibilities to perform for a church to function properly. So in some ways, when a pastor is at work, he or she is a lot like us; they get to work on time, get a cup of coffee, and start their work day. Once there, they don't just sit around waiting for the next love-starved person to walk in the door and ask to see a loving person. Neither do we. So besides the actual job requirements, their day could be much like ours. Assuming we're both dedicated followers of Christ living a life devoted to our faith, we're really not all that different. Nor should we be. They just happen to work at a church building. Certainly if anybody needed to speak to someone with a known spiritual perspective, a church would be an obvious place to start. But in reality, we are more likely to be around love-starved people during the course of our work day than the pastor sitting in his or her office.

But what if someone needed some spiritual guidance and they weren't in a church building? What if they happened to be speaking to you and brought up the same issues that would have prompted them to seek Godly, spiritual counsel in a church? If you're the real thing, you could be just as effective in getting to the heart of this person's issue as the pastor sitting in a church office.

My point is that if you truly believe in the living God, that he gave his only son, Jesus Christ, as a demonstration of the depth of his love, and you are striving daily to become the person God has always known you could be, you don't have to be a pastor to be loving. I work with a man who is actually both. Rich puts in a full day at work as a service adviser and pastors a small church east of Portland. On the weekends, he is often downtown passing out tracts and helping people find Christ. So is he a pastor or a service adviser? The label you put on him doesn't matter as long as he wears the label of believer. And whether you can quote scripture like an apostle, lead worship on a grand scale, or preach God's word with eloquence, as a believer, your most important ability must be to love. Without love, none of the rest matters all that much.

If you're a believer, your soul has a destiny of eternal righteousness. Your very salvation was purchased at a tremendous price you couldn't repay in a thousand lifetimes. Your profound acceptance of this, as you embrace Christ as your Savior, has opened your heart, your very life, to the indwelling presence of God's own Spirit. This Spirit, our Counselor, will always guide you towards righteousness and the fulfillment of the destiny God has had for you since the beginning of time. The catalyst holding this all together is God's love and it must be at the heart of all you do. With God in you, you are perpetually connected to the one inexhaustible source of unconditional love. Knowing and accepting this, you have the freedom to dispense love freely.

Here is another to way to look at it. In John 13:20 (NIV), Jesus says, "I tell you the truth, whoever accepts anyone I send accepts me; and whoever accepts me accepts the one who sent me." As a believer, as someone who accepts Christ, you are connected to God himself exclusively through the mediation of Christ and the Holy Spirit. You could call this a sort of divine hierarchy with God as the head, Christ and God's Spirit are next, followed, most remarkably, by you and me. We are not distant relatives separated by thousands of years of begetting, but as near to the ultimate Creator of all things (including love) as we are to our divine Mediator. This is part of how the "Mystery of Christ" is fulfilled in us. With Christ truly in us, we could not be closer to the source of love. It's like we perpetually have one foot in God's love aquifer. This makes us uniquely qualified to show God's love. How and if others choose to accept this love is up to them, not us. But if they do embrace the lordship of Christ for themselves, they instantaneously become a living, breathing part of God's "hierarchy." They're on his team and get to be right there in the huddle with every other believer and play from the same playbook. What is our connection with these new team mates? God's deep love for us and all of humanity-Christ living in us as members of his family, brothers and sisters in Christ.

Once we are on his team, it can start to feel like we live under a microscope. Even if non-believers don't have the foggiest idea of what being a Christian actually even means, if you're one of them, they already have their own opinion of how you should act. They don't care if you may not be having a good day. When you don't do what they expect, it conforms with the prejudged opinion they had in the first place, no matter how twisted or inaccurate it may be. The solution to this dilemma is to never do anything wrong, right? Good luck with that. It's obviously impossible. But what is possible is to let love guide you into all things. When you are motivated by the purity of love, it opens the door for God to work through you, and he doesn't make mistakes.

As believers, we are called to live lives that are Christ-like (Christian). According to a 2014 survey by the Pew Research Center, 70.6% of the people living in the United States described themselves as Christians. I'll call it a Christianity scale. With that number of people claiming to be believers, there are naturally going to be differences in the depth and commitment to living a Christ-like existence. Some people say they are Christians simply because their family has always been Christian. They might say this even if they never set foot in a church or have any kind of spiritual life. On the other end of the scale are those walking daily in a Spirit-filled life who are in church every time the doors open and remain active on a year-round basis.

But there is so much more to being a genuine believer than walking through the front doors of a church building. At best, it's a good place to start. After all, you are far more likely to worship God and have fellowship with other believers inside a church than you are at Walmart. But your decision to follow Christ, and to then follow through for the rest of your life, started in your heart and mind and that is where it resides. Stepping inside a church should only enhance and strengthen your belief. When the service is over, you take your passions home with you, securely ensconced in your heart. In John 4:24 (NIV), Jesus says, "God is spirit, and his worshipers must worship in spirit and truth." He didn't qualify his words by adding, "Oh, and your worship only counts if it takes place inside a church building."

Wherever you fall in the 70.6% of people who say they are Christian, you are also on another of scale, what I will call the "love scale." The love scale is the one that best characterizes your ability to be the loving person

God wants you to be. These two scales are not necessarily parallel. It wouldn't be impossible for someone to be at the top of one scale and simultaneously be at the bottom of the other. In other words, you might be a permanent fixture at every church service and be perceived as a rock-solid member of your Christian community yet, at the same time, really struggle to be a loving person in your day-to-day life. Conversely, you can be the friendliest, most congenial person on earth without ever setting foot inside a church, or, for that matter, even be a part of the 70.6% of people who say they are Christian. Clearly, love is capable of crossing many lines.

So why is it we can, on one hand, think of ourselves as God-fearing Christians, have meaningful, consistent interaction with other like-minded people at our churches and yet not be able, or, even more tragically, willing to act in love in our daily lives? The fact that we are human has a lot to do with it. The power of our human nature takes over sometimes. For some believers, their human nature is more prevalent than the nature of God living in them. However, as believers, I hope we all agree God's grace and loving nature in us can overcome even our most stubborn human nature. Being a Christian is an almost constant struggle between God's grace and our human nature. He wants to guide us towards his grace all the time and yet we still cling to our tendency to be our human selves. That is the mystery of "Christ in us." His indwelling presence in us is the one thing transforming our human nature into the loving nature of God, his *agape* nature.

It is Christ living in us that transforms us, be it ever slowly, into the men and women God has always intended for us to be, opening our eyes to the needs of other people, allowing us to see beyond the surface and into the heart, to make spiritual connections we may not grasp otherwise. It is Christ in us that allows, even prompts, us to smile at a homeless person or a CEO with the same motive-giving our love liberally simply for the sake of love alone, not as a necessity, but as a gift to the rest of humanity. If you are a believer, you should understand this better than anyone. God doesn't fill you with his presence and his loving essence so you can keep it to yourself. In a way, he says, "Here is my love, I will fill you to over-flowing. Give it all away. Don't worry, there's plenty more where this comes from."

Everyone is somewhere on each of those scales. Given the percentages, you are most likely part of the 70.6% who say they are Christian and you possess some ability to step outside yourself in love.

How do believers show their love? First of all, we should be sharing our love with at least as much sincerity and regularity as non-believers. But there should also be a purity in the love we believers share that could best be described as having a different source. *Agape* love, in itself, is a broad manifestation of God's love for us as his children, whether we believe in him or not. As I have clearly stated, I believe we are all born with it. As part of the human race, we should have the ability to share this type of love freely. But as believers, the love we share has a different quality, a slightly different connection to the original source-God. With Christ in us, it's like we know something others don't know yet. Let me explain. Let's suppose you're having a loving connection with someone. In the midst of this friendly exchange, besides the *agape* love you are already sharing with this other person, you could simultaneously be thinking, "This is only the beginning of love, my friend. There is an even deeper love from your heavenly Father he wants to give you freely. It is in my heart, it could be in yours." It is similar to using a two-part epoxy to bond two things together. If you use only one part of the epoxy, it will be relatively strong, but it's when you add the activator, the accelerant, that the bond reaches a whole different level of strength. The addition of God's redeeming love to our *agape* love turns it into a kind of "Super Love." This love has the unique ability to put our interaction into a different context. It's like we have taken the next step into "Perfected Love."

Don't be confused by this. The *agape* love living in us all is the culmination of every good and perfect virtue and we should all, especially as believers, be ready and willing to share it freely. But also, as believers, there is a different kind of love magnifying the significance and power of what is already part of us. And no matter how much *agape* love resides in your heart, it will never become more until you have accepted the redeeming love of Christ. When that takes place, your *agape* love has been perfected in Christ. With love of this magnitude in your heart, you should be able to step forward in strength, confidence and, don't miss this-tenderness. Remember, "Christ in you;" the perfect combination of strength and compassion.

Now comes the reality check. In spite of the perfection of God's love dwelling in us as believers, something else is rearing its head-our human nature. It really can get in the way sometimes. On occasion, it can be downright ugly. Fortunately, our Christianity provides a balance to our human nature. God gave us our nature just as much as he gave us our free will. They go hand in hand. But he also gave us the perfect solution to the disparity of our nature and his love by sending Christ into the world. The solution is the indwelling presence of his Holy Spirit living in us. When we are paying attention, when that essential spiritual relationship is functioning, it can and will override any manifestation of our human nature.

So moving forward, how do believers love others? Should it be all that different from how a non-believer loves? If anything, it should certainly be more frequent. Love, in itself, should be closer to the surface in us than in others if we are truly filled with the Holy Spirit. We shouldn't have to dig deep to access love already close at hand. In reality, love should be at the forefront of virtually everything we do. Christians, by definition, are the embodiment of Christ in this world. We are to reflect his love and truth to the rest of humanity. Therefore, acting in love shouldn't be a stretch for us.

The other side of the coin is not what we should be doing but also what we shouldn't be doing. This is the point in the story where our human nature gets tangled up with our spirituality. Here's an example of this. Have you ever had some "intense fellowship" (also known as an argument) with your spouse on your way to church? No, not ever? Okay, have you ever told someone off and used some colorful language to describe someone's lineage who just cut you off while you're driving to church (or anywhere else)? No? How about the times you intentionally avoided walking by that homeless guy you pass every day on your way to the office? Still not you? Whoa! You're really awesome. Okay, when was the last time you hugged your wife and kids and told them how much you love them?

The list of things we should be doing really is endless. And, because we're human, we're not perfect and we never will be, so a lot of those things never get done. But our humanity is not an excuse for how we choose to treat others. As believers, we should want to share the love of Christ. This gets easier as we become more and more like him throughout our lives. Of course, for this to happen, we must want it to happen and always be working towards that goal. We have to "feed" our Christianity every day. A dear pastor in my church, Pastor Updike, who has since graduated to be in God's presence, told a story about a man he had counseled. This man had struggled for years with an addiction. He characterized his struggle by comparing it to two dogs fighting inside him. The pastor asked him which one he thought would win. The man said it would be the one he fed the most. As you address the foibles of your human nature, make sure it is always tempered by your Christianity. Make sure you feed your soul daily with God's nutrition, with the right thing. Make no mistake, there are some very admirable traits in our nature. But it's when we allow God to transform us that the best parts of our nature, the ones he put in us to start with, are made better.

I do have some suggestions on what might be passing under the radar of what should or shouldn't be classified as Christian behavior. Is it okay if I use bullet points? I love bullet points. Here goes:

Do you smile a lot? It's not necessarily natural for some people. I'm not saying you have to go around with a big smile on your face all the time. However, if you greet someone (or they greet you), do it with a smile. It's a much better combination. If you have the joy of knowing Christ in your heart, don't be afraid to show it. Act like you just heard some really good news (another way of saying "gospel") and you can't wait to tell somebody.

Are you nice to your wife and kids? Think about how you are perceived in a restaurant yelling at your kids until the food arrives, and then quietly bow your heads to say grace. If your kids are just being kids, they sometimes need some help behaving, but if your public persona is one of control and dominance, you need to work on it. Remember, kids need coaches, not critics.

When you're driving your car, are you courteous? Or, do you become a monster behind the wheel? Has the following ever happened to you? You're driving along, minding your own business, when suddenly there's some guy three feet from your rear bumper screaming at you to get out of the way. When you move over and he drives by shaking his head, you notice the fish on the back of his car. Nice. There goes a great witness. It's even worse when you get to church and see the same car in the parking lot of your church. Then you realize...that's the pastor's car! Okay, that's a bit over the top. But you get my point. If you're a knucklehead behind the wheel, please do us all a favor and at least remove the fish. It would be even better if you would just not drive like that.

How are you perceived at work? Do your co-workers know you're a believer? If they don't and then find out you are, will they be shocked? "Wait. Isn't Bill the guy that got plastered at the Christmas party last year and knocked over the punch bowl?" Not good. Or consider the words of John Wooden, the legendary coach of the UCLA men's basketball team: "If I were ever prosecuted for my religion, I truly hope there would be enough evidence to convict me." When people think of you, they should know, in a good way, there is just something different about you. Do you send consistent signals about what is in your heart? In the book of Matthew, Jesus says, "For out of the overflow of the heart the mouth speaks." Does your language betray what lies in your heart? Do others know how you feel about your family? Do they even know you have a family?

At work or anywhere else, do you tell jokes that make people blush? Anything for the sake of a laugh, right? Wrong. What you say, regardless of the motivation, is, again, an indicator of what lies inside your heart. You want a Christian joke? Here's one: "Did you know there are cars in the Bible? Sure. The apostles were all in one Accord." Pretty good huh? Have you ever noticed that the best comedians are clean? Christian comedian Tim Hawkins proves this very convincingly and there are plenty of others.

Is your behavior appropriate towards the opposite sex? Do you treat the women in your life, with your wife at the top of the list, with respect and courtesy? Do you spend too much time watching a nice-looking woman walk away? Do you open doors for women? If you're a women, are your clothes appropriate? If you're a guy, do you go to church in the same sweats and T-shirt you wore when you changed the oil in your car? The old saying, "Cleanliness is next to godliness." is still valid. Do I think you should wear a suit and tie to church? If you want to. Times have changed. These days, a pastor who wears a suit is the exception. Just remember, you are going to this one particular place to worship the God and Creator of all things. Doesn't this occasion deserve some forethought about our appearance and how we act?

It's important that your behavior reflects your life of faith. You don't want to tell people you're a Christian and act like a heathen-to do so ruins your testimony. How we look, how we act, and the words we use will all contribute to how people see us. If you are the real deal, don't allow your behavior to reveal some unresolved issues in your Christian character. If you are in the presence of people you don't know, remember you only get one chance to make a first impression. Sometimes it doesn't even involve words. It's only a perception based on how you look or act before you ever even open your mouth. And if your perception with other people is good, don't mess it up when you do say something. We're going for consistency here. St. Francis of Assisi is credited with saying, "Spread the good news, if all else fails, use words." Without using words, what are you saying? Are you saying I am living my life to a higher standard? Would people be surprised to know you're a believer? When you do use words, are they the right shape, or are they round pegs jutting out of square holes?

As much as I have always liked the essence of the quote above, we, indeed, should always be prepared to use words. The Apostle Peter says, "But in your hearts, set apart Christ as Lord. Always be prepared to give an answer to everyone who asks you to give the reason for the hope you have. But do this with gentleness and respect, keeping a clear conscience..." (1 Peter 3:15, NIV). If you are a believer, you have a story, a testimony, of how God has changed your life and it's not meant to be kept a secret. Paul tells us, "For God did not give us a spirit of timidity, but a spirit of power, of love and self-confidence. So do not be ashamed to testify about our Lord." (2 Timothy 1:7,8, NIV). Every one of us has a unique story shaped by God's own hands. He intends for us to tell our story, and he's given us the tools that make it possible, so don't be intimidated by this. It's not your job to explain every miracle and point of theology to every skeptic you meet. But it is your job to share your personal story. As my pastor says, "No one can steal your story." It is your unique connection to God's story of love and redemption, and no one knows it better than you. Each of our stories has brought us to a place in our lives where we are called to be different and to live a life of purity and obedience, to live a life of loving kindness. "They overcame him (Satan) by the blood of the Lamb and by the words of their testimony." (Revelations 12:11, NIV). And our path to salvation in Christ is a different path than the world's. It is a path with unique responsibilities and expectations. And it doesn't have to be a path burdened with guilt and self-condemnation. Instead, God calls us to live a life of freedom.

Consider the words of Paul in Galatians 5:13 (NIV): "You, my brothers, were called to be free. But do not use your freedom to indulge the sinful nature; rather serve one another in love." When we accept Christ as our Savior, we have "died to sin." so we're no longer bound by its chains. But that doesn't mean we won't feel its pull. Sometimes, the pull can be significant, even to the point of hindering our hard-won freedom. Sin can never eliminate our freedom, but it can, if not properly addressed, "handcuff" our ability to move forward into all God has for us. If you're a sinner, like me, you understand perfectly well how sin's shame can exact a heavy toll capable of miring you down in remorse and self-doubt. Your enemy will never miss the chance to make the worst of this. Paul tells us to live lives of freedom, but to exercise it responsibly, being careful we don't continue to appease our sinful nature. Our freedom does not give us carte blanche to play the grace card. Instead, our freedom works to eliminate sin's "tractor beam" and allow us to soar, to live like only God could have imagined. When we are truly set free, we are free indeed to live the best part of our human nature-our loving nature, and do what it does best-to love. Given this unique freedom, wouldn't you agree God's love is worth sharing? It's your freedom, your story; don't keep it to yourself.

If you are a non-believer and you're still reading this chapter, thanks for staying with me. I hope I've opened your eyes to some of the issues we believers face as we go through life as Christians. It goes without saying we are far from perfect and, actually, I'm not so sure some are trying all that hard. Before we were believers, we were humans exhibiting every facet of our human nature, just like you. As Christians, we still have to negotiate life with that same human nature. Sometimes the train comes off the tracks. What does that prove? One thing it proves is that we're still human. But that will never disqualify or diminish the purity of what we want to be-faithful followers of the Living God. True Christians have something beating beneath the surface that sometimes gets clouded over or displaced by our humanity. But in the end, we will be able to say we grabbed on to love with both hands and all our hearts, that following Christ means more to us than trying to make the best of our human nature without Him. Do we all do it perfectly? Not a chance. Only one man ever did. There is one thing we can rest in, though: we embraced the best possible hope there has ever been for all of mankind-God's pure love.

Friends, for a moment, think of your life as a picture puzzle. Unlike the sharp image on the front of a puzzle box, the picture of who we will become is kind of blurred. The apostle Paul describes it this way: "Now we see but a poor reflection as in a mirror; then we shall see face to face. Now I know in part; then I shall know fully, even as I am fully known" (1 Corinthians 13:12, NIV). So, for our purposes, imagine the picture as a beautiful mountain stream (or whatever you find pleasing to look at). As you start assembling this puzzle, you find out quickly that in order for the finished work to look like the picture on the box, the pieces have to be put in the right place. When you try to put the right piece in the wrong place, not only does it not fit, even if you could somehow force it into place, the picture wouldn't be right. Not to mention that in some other part of the puzzle, something else will be wrong. Or could you take a piece from a different puzzle with a different picture and make it fit?

When our life is complete, we will have put some kind of puzzle together. When we're born, God is figuratively putting a box on the table. Only he knows what the completed picture will look like. The best we can do is try to make the pieces fit as they are handed to us. Every time we step outside of what God has for us, we are trying to make something fit that doesn't belong. It's when we do our best to put the right piece in the right place that we slowly become the person God wants people to see, to enjoy. When this happens, God can use us to demonstrate the best thing about us- His love in us, for us and through us.

If you are a follower of Christ, you are on perpetual "love duty." If you are confused about what love is and how to show it, stay close to your Savior. He wants you to shine in this world. If you will allow him, he'll help you put your puzzle together.

As this picture is taking shape, you are creating a lasting memory of your life and what is most important. This legacy we leave is like a monument we create with our life; a lasting memory of what God was able to do with our lives. The next chapter will help you understand the significance of this and why it must be part of the here and now.

1. How can real Christian faith shape someone into a wonderful person?

2. Do you agree with the author's belief that love has a natural connection with God?

3. What shapes the opinions of non-believers towards believers?

4. Why should a non-believer read this chapter?

5. Discuss why and how a lay person and pastor should be equally qualified to love.

6. Discuss the possible disparity between the 70.6% of people who say they are Christian and the people on what the author calls his "Love Scale". Tell the other members where you would be on both scales.

7. Do you agree with the author's belief that Christians can have a deeper form of *agape* love?

8. Discuss the list of mistakes Christians make. Could more be added to the list?

9. How does sin hinder our freedom to love?

10. Discuss the author's comparison between living a Christian life and finishing a puzzle.

10
Legacies and Love

"We will be known forever by the tracks we leave."
Dakota Proverb

My wife, Kim, is in her thirty-second year as a teacher in public schools. For the past several years, she has been teaching third grade, but she began her career with first and second graders. After so many years of teaching, she has touched the lives of hundreds of children, many of whom, by now, have third graders of their own. At the end of every day, as we discuss our days, she often elaborates on how challenging her job can be. It's a very difficult job most of us wouldn't have the patience or fortitude to endure for a single day, let alone thirty-two years. The flip-side to the challenges of her day are the victories, and there have been many.

Every year, she has at least one student who brings special challenges. This year it's a boy we'll call Johnny. Johnny is a smart kid who brings some rather aggravating personality traits to school with him. In a moment, he can go from being a relatively normal, engaged student to sitting under his desk brooding about having to write a single sentence. He has a few even more troublesome quirks I won't mention.

My wife has a choice in how she will address this student. She learned a long time ago that a defiant, dominating approach is counter-productive. Instead, she utilizes a stern, but loving approach, which tends to diffuse what could become an adversarial confrontation and, ultimately, a very difficult relationship. Johnny's first two years at school, unfortunately, were adversarial and had not produced many favorable results. Kim, of course, knew of his history. Now, four months into the school year, her approach is beginning to have some positive outcomes.

Johnny has not only made it perfectly clear he doesn't like to write anything, he has also made it known that he hates to speak in front of other people. Yesterday, one of the projects for the day was for students to write their own version of The Twelve Days of Christmas. Normally for Johnny, this would have been a fight from beginning to end. To my wife's surprise, he not only wrote the story, his story had fifteen days instead of twelve! And, he volunteered to read it, for the first time ever, in front of the entire class! But wait, there's more. When his big moment arrived, he stood in front of his peers and sang the entire song, all fifteen verses. The class gave him a standing ovation. Before the end of the day, Johnny got a ribbon from the principle and his name in the "Great Book" (I'm not sure what that is, but it sounds important).

This is but one story of how my wife has invested in the futures of her students. Every time this happens, she is making a deposit in their young lives that could lead to untold rewards later in life. Every school year, she's visited by students she taught years ago who tell her how much of an impact she made on their lives. Sometimes it's their parents telling her how she turned their children in the right direction. There is so much more to teaching than getting a child ready to pass a test. Much of the time, true success has nothing to do with a test and everything to do with sharing love and confidence to a young heart and mind.

It goes without saying my wife is not the only teacher to make some very significant contributions into the lives of his or her students. The many teachers who do this have realized that character is built one day at a time and, when the last day of the school year comes, the children are taking a part of their teachers with them. In the case of my wife and many other teachers, love and hope are the heart of the legacy they leave in every student.

As we live our lives, we get to choose what we will leave with others. What kind of a legacy am I going to leave for my family and friends? What legacy will I leave with people I may never meet? Eventually, each of us will be but a memory. Our memorial will be representative of how we prioritized our lives, the things on which we based our lives. What we devoted ourselves to will be the basis for the perception of what we were. But who we were as people will be a subjective judgment based in large part on the character and depth of the relationships we had with other people-our families, friends and colleagues. In other words, the ones to whom we were most devoted.

Most of us don't go through life dwelling on the legacy we'll leave behind. Certainly, responsible people will make provisions for a sound economic future for themselves and their loved ones and, most of us try to take care of our health. Both of these practices should be relatively basic requirements for a life well lived. We will also be remembered for what we accomplished with the time we were given. Without doubt, many of us truly have some admirable accomplishments under our belts, and, in many cases, we get well-deserved recognition throughout our lives and even beyond.

When our time on earth ends, our lives are examined more closely, and what we did and who we were will be condensed. At this point, the people whose lives we touched will have something to say about us. Have you ever heard the following statements as the only things anyone could remember about someone after their days had ended?

"She was such a good driver. She always used her turn signals and stopped at every stop sign. She had $59,372.61 in her savings and she had paid off her mortgage. And did you ever taste her grilled chicken? Simply divine! Yes, Suzanne was a pretty nice woman, but, you know...I never really knew for sure if she liked me. She was kind of different that way."

I've never heard anything like it either. Even if those statements are all true, these are not the types of things we want people to remember about us. In fact, one of the things I know I will be remembered for is my cooking. It's something I can do pretty well and it's become the catalyst for some fun and engaging times. But I hope it won't be the first thing people think of when they remember me.

I hope that when my time comes and people talk about the essence of who I was, the word love will be the first thing that comes to mind. I am equally hopeful they will know beyond doubt, that I loved and honored God and my family above all else, and that my motivation in life was to treat other people with love and respect. If you stop and think about it, is there anything else we would want to be remembered for as the foundation of our lives besides how we loved our families?

How do you think you'd feel listening to your own father's eulogy and hear the speaker say, "Bob was the president of the Fleebermayer Bank and Trust for twenty-seven years. During his tenure as president, the bank's assets rose an impressive twenty-two percent. His collection of classic cars is legendary. He is world-renowned for his collection of vintage wines and cigars. His third wife, Pixie, often said of Bob, 'What a guy.' He fathered two children, um...I have their names here somewhere. Oh, you all know who they are."

I hope you never hear anything even close. Do you want to be known for prioritizing your family, loving them more than success or money? What are you doing to build that legacy right now? Are you more concerned about accumulating stuff and feeding your ego than you are about the awesome privilege and responsibility of making sure your family and friends know they come first in your life?

Think of someone you know who openly demonstrates, above all else, that his family comes first. It's interesting to me that, when I do this exercise, the people who come to mind are usually not wealthy or influential. In fact, they seem to live fairly simple lives. But they also exhibit a carefree nature that seems to say there is a foundation in their lives sustaining them that has little to do with their bank accounts. On the other hand, I know people who are very successful and wealthy who love and honor their families. One compelling characteristic of this particular group is they are usually very generous. Even with their achievements, keeping their loving priorities in order has shaped every facet of their lives. I believe in either case, wealthy or not, early on, both groups of people made the commitment to love their families first and let the rest fall where it may.

In a culture that measures a man by his talents and achievements, the decision to love first takes courage. But it may not seem like it at first. Suppose you have been raised in a loving home and have been encouraged to be loving and considerate to other people. As you get into the "meat" of life with college, a job and marriage, you manage to maintain your loving nature. This approach has proven to fit well with where you want to go in life. Inevitably, at some point in this process of retaining your loving approach, you will be faced with decisions, sometimes small, sometimes large, that will have bearing on how well you are able to hold on to your core beliefs of putting love first. Maintaining the right balance is where it can get difficult. Let's suppose, with your career and family well on their way, you are offered a new position at work. You know going in that accepting this new position will go a long way towards a secure financial future for the people you love and cherish, but at the same time, it will require a definite shift in how much time you will have to spend away from those same people. When these decisions come along, there usually isn't much room for compromise. You either take the position and invest the time it takes or you don't. That's the way the world of commerce works. It can be a very difficult decision. You could rationalize taking the job by believing the extra time you'll spend at work will also give you more opportunities to be the same loving person to more people, or at least the same people, but for more time than you did working normal hours. Let's say you agree to take the position. It more than likely won't be the last decision of its kind you'll have to make, and each decision could have profound consequences down the road.

I am not suggesting you should never take a position that requires travel or long hours. I am, however, suggesting there should always be a proper balance. When your career comes to an end, will you be able to say you kept things balanced, or will you realize you spent too much time and devoted way too much sweat and energy in the wrong place? Will your tombstone read, "I wish I'd spent more time at the office"? If you are a praying person, decisions like these offer a good time to get some heavenly input. My wife and I would never make a career move without praying first. We live in the assurance that God, who is not only looking out for our best interests but also sees much farther down the road, will always lead us in the right direction. I can give you countless examples of how following God's lead, even when it hasn't seemed like the best decision on the surface, has worked out well for us. Sometimes, it takes a while for us to recognize it, but he has never failed us. If you aren't a praying person, you can certainly seek counsel from family, friends and associates when big decisions come along. But regardless of where your spiritual beliefs fall, your predisposition and commitment to be a loving person should always play a part in everything you do, and especially when a decision can have long-term implications.

I have tried to convince you that love can and should be a big part of who you are. Love is something we have all experienced to one degree or another. It is the only emotion that joyfully quickens our heart in so many different ways and in so many different circumstances. It can be the foundation on which we weigh decisions concerning our families, our friends and our careers. The choices we make, big or small, play a role in the legacies we leave. These choices will always at least start from the right perspective when they are flavored with love. Love's purity leaves little room for division or remorse and, regardless of how it is received, we will never regret treating every person and situation with love and respect. In the end, love can not only define our lives while we are living, but it can shape the legacies we leave behind.

Our world is made up of millions of people living their own lives, each with one beginning and one end. Each day of our one and only life should begin with the hope and expectation of being accepted with equity and respect. These are valid expectations everyone deserves. But what is the motivation for us to be fair and respectful with each other? In our world, to respect someone requires at least some amount of foreknowledge about the person. Our world says I need to get to know you before I can trust you, let alone respect you or treat you fairly. When we truly love others, we do so regardless of how well we know them. We love people and treat them with fairness and respect simply because they are members of the human race. Love allows us to see beyond those things we as humans judge with our minds. Love is a function of the heart. When we love others in this way, we open the door to the possibility of fair play and mutual respect.

What is the response to love? As I have already made very clear, there are some people who simply do not want your love, your respect, or anything else you have to offer. But I think it is a mistake to start with the assumption that everyone feels that way. If nothing comes from your attempt for positive interaction, you've lost nothing. But whether you start with the foreknowledge that your love will be welcome or not, by starting with love, you start with an opening for positive interaction. It's similar to walking into a poorly lit room. Wouldn't most of us turn on a light instead of stumbling around in the dark? Clearer vision allows us to be prepared for the obstacles in the room. Approaching the moments of your life with love follows the same principle. Love flips on the lights, so people can be prepared with a ready smile and a kind word. It's laying the groundwork before we know what's necessary, or as the saying goes, "Hope for the best, prepare for the worst."

The way I see it, when it's all said and done, the disposition of our world and the quality of our individual and collective lives boil down to two things: first, we decide how we want to live and interact with each other and second, what will make it possible. The culmination of our existence thus far surely proves that there is no end to the ways our human nature will always put us at odds. There just doesn't seem to be an end to strife and discord. But for us to go through life tacitly believing that we should, therefore, give into all of its worst manifestations is a mistake. To believe someone else will eventually figure it out will never work either.

Ultimately, each of us must choose to be productive and caring members of the world. Our free will gives us that right, that responsibility. We humans have a common core, an emotional foundation, that is able to transcend not only our human nature and worldwide cultural differences, but every facet of our social and economic lives. It doesn't need to be forced on us by our civil, societal, economic, or religious leaders. In fact, it cannot be. A foundation of love can only begin with our individual decisions to embrace our God-given loving nature and let it guide us.

Author Lewis Carroll perhaps said it best, "If you don't know where you're going, any road will take you there." I enjoy surprises as much as the next guy, but when it comes to the substance of my one and only life, a haphazard approach isn't good enough. As for me, I have chosen to embrace love. I have chosen to let love shape my life and the legacy. I hope and pray you will consider doing the same.

Am I being simplistic? Probably. But I also speak the truth. The simplicity of loving each other can level every playing field. The solution to the strife and disparity in our world doesn't have to be complicated. It doesn't have to be the result of a collection of social, economic and religious geniuses spending years of debate and study to arrive at the final solution. The solution is not only sitting right in front of us, it is already in each and every one of is. The solution is love!

Every day, we have the privilege of deciding how we will live. Even if we wake up grumpy, we can still decide to not wear the grumpy outfit. Instead, we can choose to wear something more flattering to our loving nature. We can choose an attitude that says, "I don't bite." We can accessorize with a ready smile and a kind word. We can daily choose to make a positive contribution to society. We can end our days without regrets. We can sleep well knowing we let the meaningless drama at work pass us by. And when we fail-which we inevitably do-we can start fresh the following day.

This kind of approach is not impossible. As you practice love, you will eventually begin to realize you could have been doing this all along. You may eventually ask yourself, "Why did I let all this petty stuff bother me so much?" You may find you have some new friends that really mean a lot to you. Approaching life with love is a choice you can make today. Just decide you want to experience the richness of a loving life, a life that includes the rest of humanity and its naturally interconnected qualities. When you cross paths with the guy who chose to wear his grumpy suit, you get the opportunity to show him what it could have been like if he hadn't.

For me, I will choose to wear the most comfortable clothes I own. I'm done trying to go through life wearing those scratchy, ill-fitting outfits of apathy and isolation. Should they even be in my closet? No, I got rid of mine. I suggest you get rid of yours. Fill your wardrobe with the garments of love and compassion. Wear them proudly everyday. When you see the guy wearing a burlap sack, smile and give him the name of your tailor.

Each and every day, you can choose to have a legacy of love, one destined to survive far beyond your final days. Your world, no matter how big or how small, needs you to do this, and you can. If love has been hibernating in your life, the spring thaw is here. It's time to embrace your best quality and give it free reign to change your life in ways you never thought possible. When we allow ourselves to love, our world will ultimately become a better place. Love has proven time after time that it is capable of overcoming every adversity. Every day we demonstrate that love resides in us all, that it's already there patiently awaiting our bidding. My advice to you is quite simple-let love have its way with you.

In the following chapter, I tell a story of love and how, when we allow it to be our motivation for life, good things, even great things, can happen. Love is real. Love is free, and love works every time. In fact, I believe love is freedom itself. It is freedom from the futility of hatred, apathy, and isolation. It is freedom that allows our human nature to soar and become more than we ever thought possible.

1. Discuss a former teacher who made a positive impact on your life.

2. What's the difference between what we are remembered for and who we will be remembered as?

3. How do you think you will remembered?

4. Discuss a time when you had to make a tough decision involving work and family.

5. Is there a connection between loving someone and respecting them?

6. Do you agree with the author's belief that only love can make our world what it was meant to be? If you don't agree, tell the group what would?

7. Discuss how love rises to meet adversity.

11

A Story of Love

"God does watch over us and does notice us, but it's usually through someone else that he meets our needs."
Spencer W. Kimball

As Spencer Kimball points out, God would just as soon use us, his children, to accomplish his plans for humanity. Consider how he demonstrates this in the following story.

I lost count of the number of times I'd made the trip I was about to begin. Another business trip to see the same people at the same accounts in the same towns. I would again sit across the table from the sales manager with the comb-over and the bad breath at Yorton Industries. How that guy ever became sales manager, I will never know. Maybe it had something to do with the fact that his wife's maiden name happened to be Yorton. I wonder if she has a comb over? I thought to myself. Fortunately, he wasn't the only client on my agenda.

Like it or not, it was my job to make sure my company stayed in touch with its clients, and that meant going on the road. But couldn't a simple phone call accomplish the same thing? Has this company ever heard of Skype? Apparently not. I had to make another twelve-hundred-mile round-trip journey through some of the most boring countryside I could imagine just to shake some hands and discuss the latest products from Fleebermayer and Sons. My trip would mean another week away from my wife and kids, missing yet another one of Sammy's baseball games and another week of not tucking in my three-year-old daughter, Ally. I was convinced my wife was a saint-Saint Alisha, and she was getting way too much practice at filling in the gaps when I was gone.

Despite the monotony and separation from my family, I actually enjoyed seeing many of the people on this trip. After years of calling on the same accounts, I'd developed some close friendships and, in some cases, knew more about their lives than I did about people in my own community. Yet in spite of the consistency of my visits and my best intentions, there was this one company, Self Industries, that managed to decline every sales approach. Mr. Self has always been courteous and even seemed glad to see me, but he always declined my efforts to help them expand their line.

I spent a couple of hours at the office preparing for my trip and, as I always did before every sales trip, met with Mr. Fleebermayer before leaving. Or as I would tell my wife, "I gotta meet 'The Fleeb'."

"Good morning, Sam, what's on your agenda for this trip?" Mr. Fleebermayer asked from behind his desk. Despite his position as principle owner and CEO, he was always friendly towards his employees. He knew the name of every single one and was never too busy to ask how they were doing and how their families were. This endeared him to his entire company and gave him a loyal following.

"Just letting these guys know we're still here and we still care. I do have a couple of places off the beaten path I'm going to call on, but, besides that, it'll be a fairly normal trip." I handed my itinerary across the desk. Mr. Fleebermayer briefly scanned the papers and handed them back. "What about Bob Self? Any chance of a break-through there?"

"It's hard to say. I always feel welcome there, but he seems to be pretty set on not adding any new products. Actually, he's been a bit distant the last couple of visits, like there's something bothering him. You know, not about me or us, just something else that's eating at him. I don't know. We'll see."

Mr. Fleebermayer sat back in his chair and tented his finger tips. "I've known Bob a long time. He's a good man and a smart businessman. See what you can find out. Maybe there's something we can do for him personally. I'd like to see our products in his inventory, but sometimes that's not the most important thing."

"I agree. They don't care how much you know unless they know how much you care. That's what you've always said, and it's true." We both stood. "He'll be one of my last stops, so I'll have plenty of time to think about the best approach." Mr. Fleebermayer reached across the desk, and we shook hands.

"Have a good trip and call me if you need anything."

"You know I will." I turned towards the door. Fifteen minutes later, I was pulling onto the interstate.

Five hundred miles north, a dilapidated Chevy van pulled to the side of an isolated country road. The engine stayed running, emitting a noxious cloud of exhaust gas into the cool summer night. Two men got out and moved to the passenger side. One grabbed the handle on the sliding door and slid it open. They both turned and looked up the road in both directions, making sure they were alone. Satisfied there was no other traffic, they reached into the van and pulled out a man who appeared to be lifeless. With one gripping the man under the arms and the other holding his knees, they carried the limp figure away from the van towards a fence that bordered the road. They unceremoniously tossed the man into the tall grass on the near side of the fence. The body landed heavily on its side, where it lay motionless. Without a word, the two men returned to the van. One of them noticed some pieces of the man's spare clothing in the van and flung the incriminating evidence towards the man in the grass. Thirty seconds later, the van reversed direction and sped away.

Two days passed before the man showed any sign of life. He tried to open his eyes but could only vaguely see out of one. He slowly tried to shift his position to lie on his back, but the pain was so intense, he stopped after one attempt. His left arm was loosely pinned underneath his body and, until the pain subsided, that's where it would stay. With great effort, he brought his right arm up and ran his fingers across his face. His left eye was swollen shut. He could feel something caked on his face that he couldn't identify. Hours passed in and out of consciousness.

The man awoke again. With a great deal of pain, he managed to get onto his back and free his other arm. Still in a fog, he gingerly felt his head and body to find more swelling and more pain. With his one good eye, he tried to focus on his surroundings. Minutes passed before he realized that he was lying in tall grass. With much effort, he managed to get into a seated position. Before long, he could hear the approach of what sounded like a car. Before he could stand and move any closer to the road, the car had already sped past.

"Did you see that guy back there?" The passenger said as she turned back towards the driver.

"Yes, dear," Pastor Noway said casually as he glanced in the mirror. "Probably another tweaker on a bender. They're all over out here."

"Don't you think we should see if he needs help?" Mrs. Noway asked.

"I'm sure he'll be fine. Besides, if we stop, I'll be late for my meeting with the church council. I can't be late again."

"Well, it just seems like the Christian thing to do."

"We'll see if he's still there when we drive through tomorrow."

With a great deal of struggle, the injured man managed to get closer to the road. He hoped to be more visible when the next car passed. Within minutes, he heard the sound of another vehicle approaching. Standing precariously with both hands still on his knees, he tried to focus on the drone of the approaching vehicle. As the vehicle drew near, he made out what appeared to be a large pick-up truck coming towards him. With as much balance as he could muster, he tried to raise one hand in the direction of the truck as it passed.

Inside the truck sat two young men, both gawking at the man as they passed. "Dude!" the younger exclaimed. "That's the guy from the bar the other night. Wasn't he with those two other guys?"

"Maybe." The driver returned his eyes to the road. "Looks like he had a rough night though, if he's clear out here three days later. Wonder where his buddies are?"

"Hard to say, but it's not our problem," the passenger said as he turned to face forward. "We've got work to do. That church basement isn't going to paint itself."

With his head down and his hands pressing into his knees, the injured man tried to find a comfortable standing position next to the road. When his body could no longer handle the strain, he turned from the road and, as he slowly moved towards the fence line, noticed some clothes lying nearby. He slowly shuffled over and picked them up. They seemed familiar. As he sat in the grass, he decided they would make a good pillow. Before long, he was overcome by fatigue and lay back. He tried to understand how he had gotten into this situation. No matter how hard he tried, he couldn't remember anything at all. He couldn't even remember his own name. Deep in troubled thought, he descended into fitful sleep.

The first three days of my trip had been pretty typical. Each day, I woke up early, ate breakfast and drove to the next account. It was good to catch up with old friends and meet new people. By the end of each day, I was ready for a rest in the hotel room. After my daily call home, my head hit the pillow, and I was out.

At breakfast the next day, I reviewed my schedule and realized I only had one more regular call to make. Beyond that, I was free to head up north and meet some new prospects. After, I would drive down to see Mr. Self. I met with my last regular client over lunch and set my GPS for my next stop about seventy-five miles away. By that time of the day, it was starting to get warm and the car's air conditioning made the drive more bearable and helped offset my usual tendency to get sleepy after lunch. Driving along, trying to ignore the urge to pull over and take a nap, I almost didn't see it. Out of the corner of my eye, I saw a flash of something that looked like a person laying off to the left side of the road.

"What the...?" I passed too fast, and my eyes shifted to my rear-view mirror. I could no longer see the figure so I pulled to the side of the two-lane blacktop. With no oncoming traffic, I made a U-turn and headed back. I slowed as I came near the area where I'd seen the figure and carefully edged off the blacktop, looking intently into the grass at the side of the road. There! The tires crunched to a stop in the roadside gravel. As I got out and walked towards the figure, I realized it was definitely a person, a man who appeared to be in his mid-twenties. He was lying on his side. I knelt next to him and gently touched his shoulder.

"Hey, brother. Are you okay?" There was no response. I pressed my forefingers against the side of his neck and felt a pulse. I carefully rolled him on to his back and straightened his legs. His shirt was torn and twisted on his torso. His right eye was swollen shut and his lips and cheeks were bruised and swollen. There was dried blood on the side of his head and neck. It looked like he'd been there a long time, maybe a couple of days.

"Now what?" I muttered to no one. I pulled out my cell phone. No service. I had a first-aid kit in the car, but this guy needed a lot more than what I had. Okay, Sam, think. I had to get him to a hospital.

As I was carefully putting my arms underneath him to lift him up, he began to stir and moaned.

"Hey, bud. What's going on? What happened?" I carefully brought my arms out from underneath so I could question him, find out what happened.

He slowly turned in my direction and opened his good eye. "What?...What did you say?" His voice sounded like his mouth was full of cotton balls.

"Are you hurt badly? What happened to you?" He tried to focus in my direction.

"I...I don't know. I woke up here yesterday, I think. I don't know how I got here." His voice was faint, raspy.

"Okay. I'll get some water from the car. See if you can sit up."

When I returned, he was still lying on his back. I opened the bottle of water and held it towards him. "Here, drink this slowly." He didn't move, so I knelt beside him and lifted his upper body to a sitting position. I gently poured a small amount of water between his swollen lips. His eye opened with a start, and he jerked back.

"Take it easy, bud. You're okay. I've got some water for you."

He seemed to relax and I gave him more water. He mumbled something I couldn't understand. I leaned in closer. "Sorry, what was that?"

"Thank you...for stopping."

"Of course. It's what anyone would do."

He turned his eye towards me and blinked a couple of times, then closed it.

"Let's get you on your feet and over to the car. I need to get you to a doctor." I helped him stand and, with my arms as support, we slowly walked toward the car. I opened the passenger door and guided him into the seat. "Okay, there you go. Let me tilt this seat back for you." I reached in and pulled the lever that allowed the upper part of the seat to lie back halfway. I snapped the seat-belt into the receptacle then hurried around the car and got behind the wheel. We slowly edged on to the black-top and drove towards the nearest town.

"I'm Sam. What's your name?"

The man slowly turned towards me. "I don't know."

I studied his face. Even with the swelling and obvious disorientation, I detected a hint of frustration and sorrow.

"You must have had quite a blow to the head. Do you have your I.D.?" He slowly felt his pockets and turned towards me. "I guess not. They must have taken it."

"So, who did this to you?" I asked glancing in his direction.

He spoke slowly, "I don't know. I don't remember anything. I just woke up in that grass and everything hurt. Then you showed up." He closed his eyes. I had given him the bottle of water, and he was taking occasional sips, most of which ran down the side of his face and neck.

"Well, we'll get you to a doctor and make sure you're not worse off than you look." I relaxed a bit and nudged the accelerator pedal down. We drove in silence. God, please let there be a hospital in this town.

Twenty minutes later, we arrived in the small town of Overton. The first business I came to was a rundown gas station on the edge of town. I pulled off the road and stopped next to the building. A skinny, poorly dressed teenage kid sat in a plastic chair next to the front door. Without getting out of my car, I asked for directions to the nearest hospital.

"They got one in Center City, but that's an hour away. How come you want a hospital anyway?"

"I have an injured man and he needs help right away. Is there a doctor in town?"

"There's Doc Able over on Second Street, but I don't know if he's open today." The attendant pointed towards the center of town.

"Doc Able on Second Street. Okay, is it easy to find?" I released pressure on the brake pedal and began to ease forward.

"Yeah...two blocks north and take a right. It's on the corner."

"Thanks." I called out and pulled back onto the highway.

Doctor Able's office was closed for lunch. "Closed! It's two o'clock in the afternoon. How much time do you need for lunch anyway?" My frustration was growing. I backed out of the parking area and turned towards the main road. I hesitated for a moment before turning in the direction of the next town.

"Bud," I said to the man beside me, "the doctor was closed. I'll get you to the next town as soon as I can." The man appeared to be sound asleep. His body jiggled back and forth as we negotiated the small-town streets.

As we drove from the center of town, I noticed a building standing by itself off to the right. The sign in front read, Overton Veterinary. There was a car parked on the side of the building. "What have we got to lose? Let's see if they can help." I turned into the parking area and stopped in front of the office. I half-ran to the front door, opened it, and stepped inside. At least they seem to be open for business. That was a good sign. There was no one in view inside the small office.

"Hello! Is anyone here?" I called out.

A young woman in a lab coat stepped out from the back of the room. "Oh, sorry. I didn't hear you come in." She walked towards the counter. She looked to be in her twenties. With an engaging smile, she reached across the counter. "I'm Dr. Willing. Do you have an animal that needs help?"

'Hi, I'm Sam. Um...I sort of have an animal." I hesitated. "This is going to seem kind of strange, but I have an injured man out in my car who really needs some help, and there doesn't seem to be a regular doctor available in town. Would you be willing to take a look at him?"

Without hesitation, Dr. Willing lifted the hinged end of the counter and stepped through heading towards the front door.

"I grew up in this town and I can assure you, Dr. Able is anything but! He spends more time playing golf than he does in his own office. Let's take a look." She opened the door and strode purposefully into the parking lot towards my car. I hurried to keep up with her and opened the car door. The man was as I had left him, lying back in the seat, still asleep.

Dr. Willing knelt down, leaned into the car and, after pulling a pair of rubber gloves from her pocket, snapped them on to her hands. She gently touched the young man's injuries and carefully moved his head to the side to assess the accumulation of dried blood.

"As long as he doesn't have any broken bones, as bad as this looks, it's mostly likely all superficial." She turned towards me. "Let's get him inside. Can he walk?"

"With some help. Let me see if I can get him awake and on his feet." I unbuckled his seat belt and carefully raised the seatback to a more vertical position.

"Hey, bud. I've found a nice doctor who's going to take a look at you. Can you get up?"

The man moaned and opened his eye. "What?...What'd you say?"

"I found a doctor to look at you, but we need to get you inside."

"Oh...okay." His voice was barely above a whisper. He slowly lifted his right leg and placed it outside the open door.

"Here, we'll help you. This is Dr. Willing. She's going to take a look at you." I reached in and gently helped him out of the car. With one of us on each side, we guided him back through the open office door.

We took him into an examination room and Dr. Willing carefully cleaned and assessed the man's wounds. By the time she was finished, he looked considerably better and seemed to have perked up a tiny bit. She decided it would be a good idea to take an x-ray. While she did that, I retrieved some spare clothes from my suitcase and we disposed of his old things and got him dressed.

"The x-ray didn't show any broken bones and, surprisingly, even his eye socket is intact. The worst part is the swelling, and the one deep cut. These facial contusions tend to bleed a lot and look worse than they are." She paused for a moment and, with her hands on her hips said, "Wow, somebody really did a number on you!" With her head tilted slightly to one side, she turned a bit in my direction. "The question now is, what's next? He needs a place to recuperate and, since we have no idea who he is or even what his name is, we can't very well send him home."

The young man sat on the exam table, his head intermittently nodding forward as he struggled to stay awake.

"Right. That is a bit of a dilemma." I stood for a few moments with my arms crossed and my chin between my thumb and forefinger. "Here's what we'll do. Since we don't know where he should go, I'll put him up in that motel back in town. Would you be willing to check on him every day? I'll take care of any charges. Put together a bill, and I'll take care of it. I'll make the same arrangement with the motel."

"Gosh, you're a nice guy to do that for him. I'm not worried about a bill. I've only been open a month, so I need all the practice I can get. I'm glad to help." She re-checked the bandages.

"I appreciate your willingness to look at him at all. We'll settle up when I return."

"We'll see about that." Finished, she turned towards me. "Since we don't know his name, we should give him one temporarily. How about Hugh? That's my brother's name. They actually kind of look alike."

"Sounds okay to me. What do you think...Hugh?"

"That's okay, I guess. It's better than nothing."

"Hugh it is then." I started putting my things together getting ready to leave. "So Hugh, I'm going to go check you into that motel in town, what was it called?"

"The Grace Inn," Dr. Willing answered with a smile. "It's been there a couple hundred years. Same owner I think."

"Right. The Grace Inn. So we'll check you in, and the doctor here will check on you daily. I'll have the cafe next door make sure you have water and something to eat when you're ready. Dr. Willing will give you pain medication as you need it. Does that sound okay?"

"I can't pay for that. I don't have any money."

"No worries. Don't give it another thought." I lifted my overnight bag onto my shoulder.

Dr. Willing was making some notes on a clip board. "So now where are you going to be?"

"I'm going to go up north for business. It should only take one, maybe two, days. Then I'll come back and see if we can figure out where to take Hugh. He should probably stay put for a couple of days anyway, right?"

"Definitely. He needs rest more than anything and I'll keep an eye on those wounds to make sure there's no infection. Make sure I get your cell number."

I pulled out a business card and handed it to Dr. Willing. "All my contact information is on this card. Hugh, let's get you checked into your room at the Grace Inn." We helped him off the table and made our way out to my car. When we got there, I shook hands with the doctor and helped Hugh into his seat.

"Thanks so much for your help. I'll be in touch." I waved to Dr. Willing as I drove away. The doctor smiled and waved back. I detected a spring in her step as she headed back into her office.

After getting Hugh situated in the motel, I turned back onto the highway and out of town. "Thank you, God, for that sweet angel. I knew you'd come through."

Late afternoon the next day, I pulled into the parking lot at Self Industries. I had called ahead to let Mr. Self know I was running a bit behind. He was still willing to see me for a brief meeting. I arrived at his office and, as I walked into the building, he met me in the foyer. He asked if we could meet there in the reception area. This told me it would be a short meeting so I cut to the chase.

"Thanks for seeing me today, Mr. Self. I know you're very busy." I sat on the plush sofa.

"I'll always have time for you, but today I'll have to cut it short. What have you got for me?" Before he sat in a nearby chair, Mr. Self pulled a couple of water bottles from a small refrigerator in the reception area and handed one in my direction.

I took the water bottle and opened it. "There's not much new since my last visit, but this visit may be different."

"Well, that's a relief. I'm starting to run out of excuses. What's on your mind then, Sam?"

I leaned forward and put my water bottle on the coffee table. "Please forgive me if I'm out of bounds, but, well, I mentioned to Mr. Fleebermayer that the last couple of times I've seen you, there seemed to be something on your mind, something that was distracting you. He and I both agreed that perhaps you might need someone to talk to about whatever it is." I leaned forward and, with my elbows resting on my knees, looked him in the eyes. "Is there anything we can help you with?"

167

Mr. Self sighed and sat quietly for a moment with his chin dropped slightly, his gaze fixed on something Sam couldn't see. "Tom Fleebermayer is a good man. You both are. You guys, more than anyone else, have always been genuine people and never made me feel pressured in any way." He turned his head to look at me. "I've always felt you were more interested in me than my business."

"Thank you for saying that, and you're exactly right. We do tend to put people ahead of everything else." As I looked at Mr. Self, I noticed his eyes had begun to moisten.

"You've done a good job at it." He paused, and his eyes met mine. "The truth is..." He hesitated for a moment. "I think I've lost my son."

"What! What do you mean?" My elbows came off my knees and I sat up straight.

"I haven't seen in him in a couple of months. He's always been a good kid and stayed out of trouble. But a few months ago, he started running with a couple of guys that sent all the wrong signals. At least they sent me the wrong signals. I tried to tell him, to warn him, they were up to something, but he wouldn't hear it. A couple of months ago, he said they were going to make a road trip. I tried to talk him out of it, but he went anyway. I haven't seen or heard from him since." A tear trickled down his cheek.

After hearing about his son, finding Hugh along side the road popped into my head, but that was seventy-five miles away, and besides, his son had been gone for two months.

"I am so sorry to hear that. I'm sure he's probably fine. You know how young guys can be. He'll probably show up any time with some great stories to tell." I tried to encourage him, but I wasn't all that encouraged myself.

"I hope you're right. My wife and I are going to meet with a private investigator this afternoon who says he'll be able to find him."

"That's a good idea. Well I hope your son shows up before that's necessary, but it's still a good idea to have something in place in case he doesn't. What's your son's name?"

"Todd. Todd Self. He's only twenty-six." His gaze had returned to the floor, and he took a tissue from a box on the table and wiped his eyes. We sat silently for a moment, then he glanced at his watch. "I'm sorry to cut this short Sam, but my wife should be here any minute so we can meet with the investigator. Thank you for coming by and thank you for your concern. Please give my best to Tom." He stood and extended his hand. We shook and I gave him a brief hug.

"We'll be praying for Todd. He'll show up, don't worry."

"Thanks."

When I got back to my car, I thought of Sammy and Ally and how terrible it would be if they went missing. I started the car and began my return trip. By mid-morning the next day, I was nearing Overton. I had talked with Dr. Willing a couple of times and she'd assured me that Hugh had been doing well and his spirits seemed to be improving.

I arrived at the motel and knocked on the door of Hugh's room. A moment later, the door opened slowly.

"Hey! Welcome back." Hugh greeted me with a gentle hand-shake and stood aside so I could enter. The swelling had gone down quite a bit, and he seemed to be moving more freely.

"Hugh, you look so much better! How are you feeling?"

"A lot better. Theresa, I mean Dr. Willing, has been taking good care of me."

"Theresa? You're on a first name basis? That is some progress."

"I think she's just happy to work on somebody who can talk to her without barking. She's a nice lady."

"That she is. Hugh sit down for a minute. I want to show you something."

Hugh sat on the edge of the bed and I turned the desk chair around and sat in front of him. I opened my briefcase and pulled out a couple of items and handed them to him.

"Hugh, take a look at these and see if they look familiar." I had handed him a couple of battered pieces of I.D. One was a faded copy of a gym membership. The other was a beat-up driver's license. He studied the picture on the license intently for a few moments then, still studying the photo, carefully stood and walked into the bathroom. After a few moments, he slowly walked out still holding up the license, but staring into space with a blank expression.

"It looks like me..." His gaze turned in my direction. "I think it's me." He turned his body to face me. "Where did you get this?"

"This morning, before I came back to the motel, I stopped by the place I found you and looked around. These were a couple of hundred feet away, on the opposite side of the road. I think whoever dumped you there probably tossed them out the window when they drove away."

"Then this is who I am." He walked back and carefully sat on the edge of the bed.

"Read the name on the license to me, Hugh. Who are you?"

"Todd Anthony Self. I'm Todd Self, and I live in Ready, Illinois at 2473 Safe Harbor Place. Do you think this is true?"

"Three days ago, I'm not so sure I would have recognized you as that person. Now, with the swelling down, there's no doubt. That's you, and I know somebody who will be very happy to hear about it. Excuse me, Todd, but I've got a phone call to make."

To say my trip ended on a high note would be an understatement. I barely remember driving home. I remember quite vividly reuniting with my family though. I eventually had to sit them all down and explain the tears that came to my eyes when I saw them. I told them the whole remarkable story from beginning to end. By the time I got to the end, we all had tears in our eyes.

The following Monday, I returned to work and began my usual routine after an extended business trip. I had barely started when Mr. Fleebermayer knocked on my office door. I invited him in, and he softly closed the door after he entered. He walked towards a chair with a kind of odd tip-toe step and a grin on his face. I'm sure I looked confused by his quirky behavior.

"I just got a call from Bob Self up in Ready." He sat in the chair and was leaning back with the smile still on his face.

"Oh? Is everything okay? I was going to come in and tell you about my trip later. What did he say?"

"Oh, not much. He said you had called on him, you know, the usual." He paused and fiddled with his tie. "Oh and he mentioned that you found his son, who'd been missing for two months and probably saved his life. You know, stuff like that."

"Yeah, that is quite a story. Like I said, I was going to give you the rundown later today. His son's a nice kid who got hooked up with the wrong guys. I'm glad I was in the right place at the right time, but I'm sure I didn't do anything that anyone else wouldn't have done."

"That may be, but you were there and you did do the right thing. I appreciate that. It's what this company has always stood for. It's what humanity should stand for. You had a chance to show that kid some love and you didn't miss it. Good job."

1. What are some early indications Sam works for a company that cares?

2. What would keep people from helping someone who is obviously hurting?

3. What compelled Sam to turn around and check on the injured man and then help him?

4. What compelled Dr. Willing to help Sam and the injured man?

5. Discuss Sam's motivation for covering every expense for Todd's care.

6. What gave Sam the privilege to be so forthcoming and personal with Mr. Self?

7. How was love exchanged between Sam and Mr. Self?

8. Describe the ways love touches this story from beginning to end.

9. Discuss the comparisons between Sam's story and the story of the Good Samaritan.

10. What is the significance of various names used in the story, including people and places? (Don't mind Overton. That's the street in my neighborhood).

12
Love still works

"It is better to light a candle than curse the darkness."
Eleanor Roosevelt

Sam was in the right place, at the right time. But the same could be said of the people who kept on driving. Sam was not only in the right place at the right time, he also did the right thing. Well before he arrived at that place in time, before he ever left on his business trip, Sam had already decided he would be ready to extend himself in love towards others. What he did was a natural consequence of his decision. That's how premeditated love works. Of equal significance is the fact that Sam worked for a company that operated from the same loving perspective. This defined the heart of the owner and management team and that perspective had been passed onto the rest of the employees and, eventually, to their clients.

This story, which I'm sure many of you figured out pretty quickly, retells the Biblical story of the Good Samaritan. Jesus used the story to illustrate how the religiosity of the day was missing the point of God's unconditional love. In the Bible story, the Samaritan, the one least likely in that culture to have shown compassion when compared to the two "men of God," didn't hesitate to help the injured man. The Samaritan man's loving nature, regardless of his ethnicity or position in life, overruled everything. There were no pre-conditions that interfered with what needed to happen.

I am ending my book with this story because I believe it perfectly illustrates the essence of what I have been saying. Unconditional, God-given love will always fit. It will always be the right thing at any time. There is no wrong time for love. As Sam illustrates in the story, we should be ready to love first and ask questions later. He didn't keep driving, he didn't ask a series of leading questions to see if Todd qualified for his loving help and nothing he did was motivated by an expectation of repayment or even gratitude.

While the people and events of my story are fictional, there is no doubt that over the millennia, the essence of this story has actually taken place countless times. The odds any of us will ever be put into this exact situation aren't very likely. We will, however, be given opportunities every single day for the rest of our lives to share our love in different ways. For all we know, that person we smile at may feel as if they have been discarded by life, really are hurting and lying in a ditch of lonely obscurity, bypassed by the rest of humanity, and unable to understand why no one seems willing to help.

Friends, none of us needs any special qualifications to do what I've been encouraging us to do. Every one of us is capable of showing love to each other. And no matter how contrary it may be to your nature, to your station in life, or to your perception of how our world should function, love could change our world into a place that welcomes and celebrates our differences, that sees beyond apathy and back into the loving heart beating in every one of us.

Every year at Christmastime, churches all over the world include candlelight services as part of their celebrations. The church I attend is one of them. With the sanctuary lights turned off, Pastor Remington lights the candles of several people standing in the front rows. These people, in turn, light the candles of a few people standing near them. In this manner, every candle in the sanctuary is lit. The pastor will then ask us all to raise our candles over our heads for a moment. This sight of well over a thousand tiny lights, especially when accompanied by beautifully played music, is inspiring almost beyond words. For me and many others, it is the pinnacle of our Christmas celebration. I have experienced many candlelight services, and each time, my heart swells with thankful joy.

It always amazes me how a totally darkened room can be transformed into to a well-lit space. When the flame has lit every candle, the room has enough light to see each face. All of this illumination and the emotions it stirs began with one solitary person holding one solitary candle. Obviously, without the first candle, none of the other candles would have been lit. We all would have remained in the dark.

I'm not sure I can think of a better way to illustrate what this book is about. For me, the flame of that single burning candle represents the glow of love that burns in each and every one of us. No doubt, it burns a little brighter in some of us than in others, but love's embers never go cold. We all have love's "pilot light" burning inside. So, with that in mind, let's pass on the flame and light candles.

Our world desperately needs a candle light service!

Will yours be the flame that brightens your corner of the world? Are you willing to light some candles in your own family, in your circle of friends, at your job, on your way to work, or wherever you happen to be?

Love is the singular best thing we all have in common, and it burns in each of us. If we are willing to let our love touch the life of another, if the ones we touch do the same, I am convinced the troubling path leading us towards disconnected apathy, selfishness, and isolation will begin to shift. Every loving connection will add light to our path until it becomes brighter and broader and begins to resemble a meadow more than a path. In the brightening light of this ever-widening space, our lives will be connected as they were meant to be. We will be able to turn full circle and discover we aren't alone after all. We matter to each other. The darkness that would like to have its way with our cultures, our societies, with the very world in which we all live will have no place to hide. Love alone can do this. It sits inside each of us, ready to do what it does best-to be given away.

Love will always win. Please don't miss it.

1. How does the final chapter encapsulate the essence of not missing love?

2. Who are the people in our lives, our world, who need a Good Samaritan?

3. Discuss how a Christmas candle-light service demonstrates how love can be shared.

4. Summarize your experience reading Don't Miss Love.

5. Relate examples of how you may have started to share the principles of this book.

6. If you are a non-believer, what is your take on the author's spiritual connection between love and God?

7. Do you agree with the author's belief that love can be the catalyst for a better world?

8. If you could ask the author any question, what would it be?

9. Will you share the ideas and beliefs of Don't Miss Love with others?

10. Finally, are you glad you read this book?

Epilogue

I began writing this book early in 2016. Since then, there have been some significant developments in my life I feel are worth mentioning. I stated in the opening chapter I had been treated for throat cancer. More specifically, I was treated for squamous-cell carcinoma, alias Base of Tongue cancer. I finished the treatment in September of 2015 and was declared cancer-free in December of that year. Unfortunately, as cancer sometimes does, I was told in the early summer of 2016 it had metastasized. At that time, it appeared to be incurable, inoperable stage four cancer residing in my lungs and upper body. Since then, I have undergone three clinical trials. The first two proved to be ineffective. But the third appears to be working. With God's gracious touch, that will continue.

I am adding this information because I believe anyone who has devoted the time to read and consider the content of my book will have a sense of how important the subject of love is to me. I seriously doubt I would have written the book if I had not gotten cancer in the first place, not because love didn't matter to me before, but because, with cancer, I started looking at life differently. My priorities changed. Since the diagnosis, my whole life has changed dramatically, and this is in addition to the obvious changes cancer brought to my life. When your mortality enters the picture, you start to thin out the fluff and figure out what really matters.

After spending a lot of time on my practical, emotional and spiritual vetting list, I realized that love kept ending up at the top. Everything else was relative to love. Instead of trying to see love in all the various aspects of my life, I realized love itself was giving me a perspective that measured the significance of everything compared to love. In the end, love won every contest. Love, more correctly, God's love, has taken over every part of my life. My cancer? It's almost like a part-time job I would just as soon not have, but am forced to go to once in a while. Actually, mostly due to the return of cancer, I retired in July of 2016. So my treatments really are the closest thing I have to a job. One big difference, however, is that I have to pay for the treatments and they're not cheap. The extra time did allow me to finish the book sooner, so it's been worth it.

Another event occurred about a few months ago that put a very fine point on the significance of love. Our dog, Toby, passed away. He had been pretty healthy for most of his thirteen years and, really, just had one bad day-his last one. Now, a few months removed from that sad day, we are recovering. Think what you want, but I believe I will see him again. Why would God leave out one of his very best examples of unconditional love from eternity? I don't think he will. Here's another thing I believe about dogs and eternity: there will be no shovels in heaven (too much gold pavement).

So, you now know where Steven Batchelor stands after writing what I truly hope will be a book capable of improving at least a few lives. My best expectation, my honest and fervent prayer, is that many people will embrace love as I have. It has, almost single-handedly, turned my life from one that could quite understandably have been filled with doom and gloom into a life of happiness, hope, and joy-real joy! God's unrelenting love flavors every single day I have with a richness I had never known before, and whether I live twelve more years or twelve more months, I am happy to be where I am and to have had the opportunity to share something so precious with you.

Thank you so much for reading my book. I truly hope it has blessed you at least in a small way. My greatest hope is that it has not only blessed you, but has opened a world that brings a smile to your face and quickens your heart every day.

May God bless every single day of your life.

ABOUT THE AUTHOR

Steven Batchelor is recently retired from a career in aviation and the automotive service industry. He is a first-time author, accomplished artist and guitar player. He and his wife, Kim, live in Portland, Oregon. If you enjoyed this book, please consider adding a review on Amazon. Thank you. Look for Steven's next book, *The Exploding Toilet and Other Stories of God's Grace*, in fall, 2018.

Made in the USA
Middletown, DE
16 July 2020

12911802R10109